253

G. Lewis

D0990607

EMMANUEL
SCHOOL OF RELIGION
LIBRARY

THE ART OF CONDUCTING
PUBLIC WORSHIP

THE MACMILLAN COMPANY
NEW YORK · BOSTON · CHICAGO · DALLAS
ATLANTA · SAN FRANCISCO

MACMILLAN AND CO., LIMITED
LONDON · BOMBAY · CALCUTTA · MADRAS
MELBOURNE

THE MACMILLAN COMPANY
OF CANADA, LIMITED
TORONTO

American Seating Co. photo.

First Presbyterian Church, Topeka, Kansas, before and after remodelling

THE ART
OF CONDUCTING
PUBLIC WORSHIP

Albert W. Palmer
President of The Chicago Theological Seminary

THE MACMILLAN COMPANY

New York : 1939

EMMANUEL
SCHOOL OF RELIGION
LIBRARY

BV
10
. P23

39-7283

Copyright, 1939, by
THE MACMILLAN COMPANY.

All rights reserved—no part of this book
may be reproduced in any form without
permission in writing from the publisher,
except by a reviewer who wishes to quote brief
passages in connection with a review written
for inclusion in magazine or newspaper.

Set up and printed. Published March, 1939.

FIRST PRINTING.

PRINTED IN THE UNITED STATES OF AMERICA
AMERICAN BOOK—STRATFORD PRESS, INC., NEW YORK

Purchase

R. O. Roberts

12/23/67

Dedicated to the memory of

WALTER RAUSCHENBUSCH,

whose Prayers of the Social Awakening
have helped so many to pray with renewed
purpose and mystical devotion.

And to

GEORGE A. JOHNSTON ROSS,

gift of Scotland to America, who taught men
how to preach and worship and face reality
unflinchingly. In the noblest sense a prophet,
priest and, above all, a friend.

6280

Acknowledgments

This book could not have been written without the help of many known and unknown friends. I am especially indebted to two members of the staff of The Chicago Theological Seminary, Miss Marjorie Brown and Miss Marjorie Hovey, who did the typing; to the American Seating Company for the pictures of church interiors; and to Mr. Bruce Porter, Mrs. Ozora S. Davis, Rev. James Morrison, Rev. J. M. Spence, Rev. Hénry S. Lieper, Rev. Raymond Calkins, E. P. Dutton and Company, Willett, Clark and other owners of copyrighted material, for permission to use excerpts and quotations. Two members of the faculty here at the Seminary, Professors Pauck and McGiffert, have been helpful in reading and criticising the manuscript. I am grateful to Rev. E. S. Freeman for ideas concerning the Lord's Supper and to Professor Fred Eastman for his suggestions on church lighting; also to my students and members of my own family who listened to the reading of portions of the manuscript and offered helpful suggestions. But, of course, all responsibility for any errors in fact or judgment, is mine alone.

ALBERT W. PALMER

CHICAGO THEOLOGICAL SEMINARY
February 12, 1939

Contents

Illustrations

The Necessity of Miracle

THE CONDUCT OF PUBLIC WORSHIP is probably the weakest point in the ordinary protestant church. Partly because it is often so poorly done, and therefore capable of such immediate and prompt improvement, it presents just now a very strategic opportunity for advance. People need exactly what a well ordered worship service can bring to them and this deeper and richer religious experience will be increasingly needed as life grows more tense, exacting and complex. Moreover, is not the best way to meet the current tendency toward declining church attendance the provision of a worship service which does so much for people that they cannot afford to stay away from it? The services of the church are subject nowadays to competition never known before. Radio, movies, the automobile and the paved road, the Sunday paper and illustrated magazine, modern pagan tendencies in life and thought, and, above all, the need for letdown, relaxation and change after the strenuous life of the week, all combine to keep people from going to church. On the other hand, they will go miles and put up with many inconveniences in order to see or share in something which ministers to real needs and inner hungers. In the conduct of religious services the church has no competitor. Worship is religion's unique function, and, properly conducted, it can win more people than lesser things can lure away.

There is no enduring religion without miracle. It will be only because men find religion doing for them what they cannot do for themselves that they will turn to religious worship. Our modern age, with its emphasis on science and its quest for a rational explanation of everything, has too largely lost its sense of the miraculous. Modern Biblical scholarship has sharply reduced or even eliminated the miraculous element in the Bible. Current scientific methods of investigation have seriously impaired the immediate force and credibility of miracles which are dated hundreds of years ago. What we need is a contemporary miracle! And worship can provide this! For most Protestants at least, this cannot be the transubstantiation by which bread and wine are literally transformed into the actual physical body and blood of Christ. But that, even in Catholic circles, is secondary to what happens to the believer who accepts it. The real miracle of worship is the actual spiritual communion with the divine which may take place, the imparting of transforming peace and power to jangled, beaten, discouraged lives. A worship service into which people have come troubled, defeated, doubtful, and out of which they go with hearts again uplifted and countenances aglow, ready to meet life with new courage and deeper insight— such a worship service has performed for them the most convincing of all miracles. A church that can work contemporary miracles in people's lives by its worship services will not be ignored or neglected.

This book is written in the hope that it may reveal why such miracles are not wrought oftener and how the art of working them can be regained. If anyone says, in a critical mood, that worship is something offered to God, and not something done in behalf of man, I can only fall back on Jesus' great word about the Sabbath, that it was made for man. In like manner must we not believe that he who taught men to pray would approve a recognition of the healing, comforting, creative power of prayer as in no sense derogatory of its value and meaning to God? Worship is, of course, a duty to God, as any reverent and thoughtful man must recognize, but, like all other duties well and cheerfully performed, it also beomes in turn a help to man.

As the book unfolds it will be quite obvious to the reader that it has in view not the problems of Episcopalians and Lutherans but of so-called free churchmen. The problems of the liturgical churches are in a class by themselves. This book does not pretend to deal with them, but seeks rather to help the non-liturgical church of the puritan background and tradition, whether Congregational, Baptist, Presbyterian, Methodist, Disciple or of some other denomination. And it seeks to be a book not primarily of academic research and technical detail but of broad outlines, working principles and practical illustration, equally interesting to the thoughtful layman, the choirmaster and the pastor.

CHAPTER ONE

Where Worship Fails Today

THE SUCCESS OR FAILURE of a worship service may be measured by three questions: First, is it a sincere outreach toward God and an act of real self-dedication on the part of the leader and the worshippers? Second, does it hold attention and command respect and participation by the congregation? Third, has it inherent qualities of beauty, dignity and artistry which will appeal to all in proportion to their ability to judge and appreciate? Does it, in other words, make adequate and effective use of sound psychology, recognized liturgical principles, good music and the vast treasurehouse of worship material in the Bible, in the world's devotional literature and poetry and in the resources of symbolism, color, movement, architecture, lights and silence? Surely anyone responsible for the conduct of a service of public worship will not be content with any ideal less than the full attainment of all of these three standards.

Modern worship probably does not often fail because of insincerity. The worldly dissipated fox-hunting parson of the eighteenth century is practically never encountered today. Our worship breaks down, not because of the hypocrisy of the clergy but because of sheer lack of interest on the part of the congregation. And this, in turn, is due to lack of knowledge and skill in the art of leading worship on the part of ministers and choirmasters. Integrity of

4

character and deep sincerity of purpose on the leader's part are basic and absolutely indispensable requirements in public worship. No outer thing, no grace, no art, no learning, can ever be substituted for these inner and primary essentials. But integrity and sincerity are not, in themselves, enough. The congregation also must be interested and eagerly coöperating to make the service a success. "He's a sincere man but awfully dull!" or "The poor fellow means well but I can't stand his mannerisms, or his voice, or his slovenly way of conducting the service!" Such reactions as these are driving people away from churches manned by perfectly honest and devout pastors.

Wherein, then, do our protestant services so often fail to arouse the interest and hold the attention of the congregation? Let us be very definite here and list the shortcomings of our worship service with such stark realism that we may face them without evasion. All the rest of the book will be concerned with the problem of what to do about these five cardinal sins against the spirit of worship.

1. *Lack of Impressiveness and Solemnity*

Impressiveness and solemnity do not mean gloom or depression. A service does not have to be funereal or move with a dirge-like tempo to be impressive. But it does need order and dignity in setting, plan and content. The trouble is that so often our church services lack the meaningful and stately movement of a procession and are more like the aimless strolling of sightseers along a Florida side-walk. This is partly because of the background. The architecture is sometimes trivial or even violently atrocious, the arrangement of pulpit and choir-loft scattered and disharmonious, with no central focus for attention except the organ pipes or, worse yet, the organist bobbing about on a high bench in the active quest of stops and pedals and in full view of the congregation. There is no great symbol of religious faith on which the mind can focus its attention—nothing but the organ and the self-conscious whispering choir and, perchance, the top of the minister's head just visible above the pulpit as he sits, sometimes too conspicuously for all not in line with the pulpit, and sometimes hidden like an exotic tropical animal in the midst of a jungle of palms, potted plants and flowers. The Bible on the pulpit which, if large and reverently displayed, might have provided a noble bit of symbolism, and once did in former generations, is now hidden behind an acousticon or has disappeared altogether while the minister reads the impressive words of scripture rather casually from an unimpressive little pocket testament.

Not only is the setting unimpressive but the service itself too often has a quality of improvisation about it. It begins at no beginning and it moves to no end. Especially is this so if the minister is obviously hunting for hymns in the hymn book or fussily leaving the pulpit for a consultation with the organist or some last-minute instructions to the ushers. Add to this the buzzing conversation by the congregation, the variegated display of dress and millinery by the choir, the minister's brown shoes, brilliant socks, red necktie and over-prominent watch charm, the glass of water on the pulpit and the Sunday School call-bell and a few dog-eared quarterlies absentmindedly left on the communion table, and you have a picture of one reason why church services sometimes fail to impress the congregation or hush them into an attitude of reverence and awe.

2. *Poverty of Material Used*

Even in so bad a setting, great material nobly used might still avail to save the day. But here again our services often fail to make full use of the treasures that are available. The Bible selections may be carelessly chosen and poorly read, no effort being made to secure variety and a knowledge of the great classical passages of scripture. There is no carefully selected series of readings opening up the Bible and revealing its many-sided wisdom over a period of weeks or months. The responsive readings also are either too long or contain unedifying verses from the imprecatory psalms and, at best, are only a practice in the alternating reading of verse and verse about by pastor and people without any dramatic division of content between what the minister reads and the congregation responds.

Litanies, responses and other liturgical forms will be largely absent and the whole wealth of extra-Biblical Christian devotional literature undrawn-upon. If there is a confession of faith it will be the Apostles' Creed. But this may be omitted through fear that it will raise difficulties for important groups in the congregation, students, teachers and others, through its reference to the virgin birth and the bodily resurrection. In this case, however, the unifying experience which a sonorous confession of faith might have served in drawing the congregation together is lost.

Along with the decreasing use of such a verbal symbol of our common Christian faith there is an absence of any great visual symbols. A cross may be inconspicuously worked into a stained glass window but will not be welcomed on the communion table. The walls will be decorated with fresco designs like unto those in the moving picture theater down the street and the communion table may be absent or reduced to an inadequate little stand below the pulpit.

And the prayers! Will they echo the great words of scripture and have overtones from the hymns and devotional literature of the ages, so noble and searching that a hush comes upon the people as the minister uplifts their souls with his before the mystical presence of God? Will they be such prayers, or will they be casual, improvised, rambling and one-sided, leaving great areas of spiritual need untouched?

3. *Lack of Unity*

Have you ever observed some protestant congregations assemble for an eleven o'clock service? A few hardy souls are there ahead of time. If the service begins on time, from one-third to two-thirds of the potential congregation greet the minister as he surveys the scene. The doxology is sung and a few more drift in. After the responsive reading another contingent arrives. The children's sermon is now over and, at a point indicated by stars on the bulletin, the ushers seat a large well-dressed, important-looking delegation; a few more arrive even after the collection is taken up, though that is not considered really sportsmanlike. But by the time the sermon begins everybody who is coming is expected to be on hand. No wonder the Scotch minister prayed for "those of the congregation who are here, those who are on the way, and those at home who may come but haven't yet made up their minds"!

Why this diversity in time of arrival at a service which begins at eleven o'clock? May it not be largely because of the lack of any sense of unity in the service? That pathetic phrase, "the preliminary exercises," still occasionally used to describe the worship service before the sermon, may have gotten so deeply into people's minds that they think they can arrive at any time while these exercises are still going on and not feel tardy. You can afford to miss the previews, the news flashes and the animated cartoon if you arrive in time for the six-reel feature—which is the sermon! A series of separately announced events, now a hymn, now a prayer, now a reading, now something else, all arranged in no psychological order and utterly lacking in unity does not make an effective worship service.

4. *Musical Shortcomings*

It is in the field of church music that many a protestant church spends more and gets less for its money, so far as any worshipful values are concerned, than in any other part of its program. The worst thing about our church music is apt to be not its quality but the location of the singers and the concert psychology which results therefrom. Perch a lot of people up in serried rows behind the minister and under the constant gaze of the congregation, and then have a director stand up on a stool beside the pulpit with his back to the congregation, coat-tails flying, and wave a baton at the choir with all the fervent gyrations of an orchestra director, and you may have a concert but hardly a service of worship.

We do not need to pause to deplore the poor quality or over-ornateness of the music so often sung, but pass on to

the over-emphasis on the anthem and the failure to realize
the values of responses and versicles which might have
bound the items of the service into unity and helped to create a sense of peace and aspiration. Instead, these seemingly
unimportant because modest elements in the music of the
service are forgotten and too much attention concentrated
on the rendering of one or more anthems. After which the
choir sits down and fans itself, the congregation engages in
active musical criticism, and the minister tries to gather
things up as best he can and get forward with the service
once more!

5. *Congregational Non-Participation*

Deeper than any of the evils yet listed, bad as they are,
is the persistent attitude of non-participation on the part of
the congregation which not infrequently characterizes the
protestant worship service. In the famous dispute which the
Puritan divines had with the Anglican bishops in 1661,
Charles II being the umpire, the Puritans objected to responses and litanies because they argued that it was the
prerogative of the minister to conduct divine worship and
the laity ought not to encroach on this beyond meekly saying "Amen" after the prayers. Well, in most churches of
the Puritan tradition the congregation has even stopped
saying "Amen"! This non-participation is evident in pos-
ture. There is a lamentable tendency for people to sit bolt
upright and even gaze about during the prayers. And it is
also manifested in half-hearted participation in the repetition of the Lord's Prayer, the responsive readings and
even the singing of the hymns. I have conducted services
where it seemed as if the congregation were only there as

spectators, coldly and critically sizing up the minister to see how good a performance he could put on! The Catholics have a valuable phrase, "to assist at mass," as descriptive of the function and attitude of the congregation in attendance at the worship service. Altogether too few occupants of protestant pews have any such attitude. They feel they are there to be preached to (or at!), but have a far less definite sense of sharing in the conduct of the service.

Why is this? In part, at least, it undoubtedly grows out of the traditional type of church service in which the congregation has had too little active participation. This is particularly unfortunate, not only because it naturally reduces their interest in the service, but much more because it deprives them of a religious experience. The thrill of saying great words and using deeply religious language is something which people with our modern inhibitions peculiarly need. As Dr. Raymond Calkins has wisely pointed out, "There is all the more reason for embracing this opportunity (for active participation in the liturgy) at the hour of common worship because of the difficulty which many people recognize of speaking about the reality of religion in private. A feeling of reserve, due in part to reverence, but also in part to false timidity or downright lack of personal conviction, keeps them from uttering in personal ways during six days of the week the faith that is, or should be, in them. All the more reason, therefore, for uttering in corporate fashion, on the first day, their common faith at the hour of common prayer and worship."[1] As the Psalmist puts it: "Let the redeemed of the Lord say so"!

The overcoming of this all too common attitude of de-

[1] *Concerning Public Worship. Letter No. 6.* April, 1930.

tachment and aloofness from any active sharing in the worship service is one of the principal objectives of this book. But one suggestion, not liturgical in character, which has been made by a friend of the author, may well be inserted here. It is that the general vitality of the church as an active, well organized body is basic to any solution of this program. People are more apt to enter actively into the worship service of a church in which they are also engaged in doing other things actively, too. Get the members of a congregation to doing something for others under the banner of the church and they are more apt to stand at attention, and even cheer, when that banner is raised on any public occasion. But, if the church invites them to do nothing but worship under her auspices, the chances are they will not do even that very well.

If this chapter seems unduly critical and largely negative the reader is asked to remember that its purpose is more provocative than constructive. It seeks to reveal alarming symptoms and hint at diagnosis rather than indicate the treatment involved. Simply let me say that while all of the shortcomings listed, fortunately, are not concentrated in any one local congregation, all of them do exist and have actually been observed in recent months as the author has gone in and out among churches of all denominations, east and west.

The hopeful thing is that there is an almost pathetic desire for better things. This results, oftentimes, in effects being sought without knowing how to go about securing them in the wisest way. Undesirable and even tasteless "enrichments" of the service are lugged in. Take the matter of candles, for instance. Having deprived ourselves of the beautiful symbolism of the lighted candle for centuries, we have suddenly recovered it and are finding, to our great joy and relief, that we can now use candles on the communion table without becoming Roman Catholics overnight. So what do we do? Put two symbolic candles on our table? Nothing so tame as that! In the exuberance of reaction from three hundred years of luminary deprivation we install one hundred and twenty-one candles in the chancel of one small church! I counted them!

If this tendency to go to extremes and occasionally do liturgically desirable things unintelligently needs to be listed among the shortcomings of contemporary worship services, it is at least a hopeful shortcoming. It tells of vitality and of a creative drive toward better things. Out of its uninstructed exuberance, will emerge shortly a new vitality and power in public worship.

CHAPTER TWO

The Theological Assumptions of Worship

WHAT WORSHIP MAY MEAN to God we have no way of knowing. And yet we must have faith that it is not without meaning for God, just as no other significant activity in the universe can be meaningless to him. Probably a profounder worship experience, like a nobler social order, as was so impressively brought out in the Oxford and Edinburgh Conferences of 1937, waits on the achievement of a better theology. The basic thing that is the matter with the age in which we live is that it has no adequate, generally accepted and authoritative theology. When our sense of God becomes at last contemporaneous, vivid and intellectually approved, marvelous things will begin to happen in every department of human life—economic, social, international, and especially in the areas of personal religion and public worship.

This book is written on the foundation of a very simple but definite theology. The author believes in God. He conceives of God as that invisible ever-present and inescapable unifying power by which the universe is created and constantly upheld, renewed and carried forward. That there is such an integrating force pervading all the facts of life seems to him the only satisfactory rational conclusion from our personal experience, the records of history, the results of scientific research and the balanced judgment of philosophy.

Not only is there a God, but, in view of the marvelous and intricate adjustments of the universe, that God must be supremely intelligent. The highest intelligence with which we are in contact is the human personality. Therefore we feel sure that God must be in some sense personal. We must, of course, be careful not to imprison him within the limitations of human personality and we cannot, therefore, think of him as just a glorified human being. But, on the other hand, a universe which has flowered forth into personality with its intelligence, creative power and capacity for love and beauty and moral choice, can never be adequately accounted for on a sub-personal or non-personal basis. Whatever incomprehensible more there may be, there must at least be personal qualities in God. God can be apprehended only in part through the laws of nature and the activities revealed by a study of physics, chemistry and biology. The splendor of order and beauty in the starry heavens above and the orderly processes of mathematics may tell us much about God, but, as Kant recognized long ago, the moral law within the soul of man also has to be accounted for. Man, too, is a fragment of the universe and what he is and aspires to be is part of our evidence concerning the nature of God. In view of the fact of human personality God must be superpersonal, not sub-personal or impersonal, if we are to be moved to worship him.

Especially is this true when we consider Jesus Christ as humanity at its best and highest. We may protest against an extreme Barthianism which refuses to see any revelation of God except in Christ, ignoring the cosmic order, the on-going creative drama of evolution, the insights of saints and sages through all the centuries, and finding God revealed only in the brief historic life of Jesus of Nazareth. But let us also beware lest we, on our part, neglect or undervalue the profound significance of the fact of Christ. If personality is the most marvelous thing we know in all the universe, then Christ, as our sublimest, purest, most perfect personality, is of supreme importance as revealing to us the qualities which we feel must also be in God. Must there not be something Christ-like at the heart of a universe which has blossomed forth in the life of Jesus Christ? It is no mere idle fancy or mechanical formula, then, when we pray "in Jesus' name." It means that here in Christ we feel sure the veil is thinnest between the human and divine and that God was in Christ reconciling the world unto himself.

For those to whom it means the most, worship is, therefore, essentially an overt and conscious act based upon a profound conviction as to the reality of God, and for Christians, it is, in addition, a feeling that Christ is a very special and supremely important revelation of that reality.

But it is more than this. Worship makes one great and sublime assumption, namely that God is conscious of man and that man's hopes, fears, aspirations, gratitude and even requests can register themselves upon the consciousness of God. And this registration takes place not through the sounds that man makes, which are pitiably short-ranged and inadequate, nor is it accomplished by the motions he goes through on the level of physical activity. Rather it must be essentially through the unseen and unheard agitations of his consciousness that man's worship touches and affects the cosmic consciousness of God.

This, of course, leads straight toward mysticism. But mysticism, as I use the word, is not something occult, uncanny and irrational but rather something super-rational, akin to the super-personality of God. Mysticism is simply the leap of faith which we must take if we are to commune with God in worship. It is the sublime assumption that there is in the universe not only the physical inter-related unity which the natural sciences assert and largely demonstrate but also a spiritual unity and an inter-related consciousness in which we all share but of which we are not all equally aware and of which God is the central unifying factor. The physical analogy of radio with its central broadcasting station sensitive to and received by innumerable individual radio sets the world around, helps to make such a conception acceptable and intelligible to the modern mind.

That this is no idle fantasy is demonstrated by what happens to those who worship in spirit and in truth—and also by what happens to those who are color-blind or stone-deaf to these spiritual influences and who never make any response to them, if indeed there be any such completely earth-bound personalities. What worship may do for the worshipper will be taken up more in detail in the next chapter. Here we simply note that it does do something for him and what it does is vitally related to his faith in the object of his worship, which is God. I would like to keep the door of worship with its cleansing and stimulating power wide open for everyone, no matter how vague, inadequate or incoherent his conception of God may be. Even though he define God very abstractly as simply anything that has supreme value, still he can be a worshipper. All worship, except self-worship, can be included. Worship, indeed, in its etymological origin, means worth-ship, the recognition of value. But, obviously, the greater, clearer, more awe-inspiring one's conception of God becomes, the richer and deeper the worship experience will be.

Here we are, conscious, questing human beings, set amidst the splendor, order and tragedy of the universe, capable of comprehending something of its intricate and yet marvelously adjusted creative pattern. Before us the sunsets come and go and all the pageantry of heaven and the changing year. All this external world has meaning because of something within us which has consciousness, is sensitive to values, has artistic and creative power, seeks for truth, feels the power of music, sacrifice and moral ideals and cannot rest until it finds some unity and meaning in it all, until, as St. Augustine put it, we rest in God. The great majority of men are so objectively minded that all they see is the outward pageant of life. Their feelings, emotions, intelligent interpretations and spiritual hungers, are conceived of as something apart from reality, almost to be apologized for, certainly not particularly important. But what if these emotional needs and spiritual hungers are, after all, really a part of the pageant, perhaps the most important part, without which the external events are colorless and meaningless? Then, thought, emotion, quest for truth, interpretation of outer phenomena, moral judgments, love, self-sacrifice, heroic loyalties, become realities, the highest realities of all. They, too, are part of the universe. God must be in some vital sense related to them. He is not only a God of chemistry and physics, of sunsets and distant stars, of blind vegetation or animal automatisms. We suddenly become aware of him as the source of consciousness, of thought, value, aspiration, love, morality, creative passion. He is the God of our highest selves, not merely of our semi-mechanical bodies! Then, what it might mean to worship! How we should turn to such a God as to a great friend, as to one who is indeed the Father of our spirits, sharing with him all we are and hope to be and waiting in high exultation for the joy and thrill of a divine comradeship! A nobler worship experience waits on the recovery of a sense of God as contemporary, spiritual and accessible. When enough people experience God, not only in the outer world, but in their own inner lives as well, worship will be reborn. Worship awaits a new sense of religious mysticism.

Meanwhile worship suffers from being bound, in popular conception, to outmoded and, for modern men, impossible theological conceptions. It is paying the penalty for the outgrown theology of the past. Men stay away from worship, or tolerate it with a resignation akin to resentment because they have renounced the theology which it implies or which, at least, they assume it implies. Here we ought to clear the decks. Worship, while to reach the heights it must use the language of personality, should free itself from the anthropomorphisms found both in the Bible and the prayer-book. It must root down into as universally appealing theological conceptions as possible. Great philosophical assumptions about God and the spiritual nature of the universe must, of course, undergird all worship. But worship, while it has theological foundations, had better avoid theological details and keep itself hospitable and comprehensive enough so that men of various theologies can still worship together.

It will be particularly helpful if the conception of prayer, which is the central act in worship, can be released from its too exclusive emphasis upon petition. Not that petition should be excluded. We need to ask the universe for something. Prayer will lose much of its tang and reality and probably wither away if our theology is so dominated by mechanistic determinism that we cannot ask for anything. But after all there are many other sides to prayer. There is the prayer of thanksgiving, greatly needed in a hurrying self-sufficient age, the prayer of praise, the prayer of adoration, the prayer for spiritual companionship, for enlightenment, harmony and communion. And there is the prayer of dedication. As Dr. Fosdick has suggested, our prayers should be "use me" oftener than "give me." When all these sides of prayer receive due recognition then the prayers of intercession and petition fall into place and do not unduly obtrude themselves. Dean Sperry has called attention to the fact that the prayers in the Jewish liturgy are very largely prayers of thanksgiving and of recognition of the greatness of God.

Sometimes, too, it will help bind worship and theology together if we can get away from the familiar stereotyped phrases to language which is refreshingly real and even startlingly contemporary. I shall never forget the thrill that came to us all one day in the vesper service at The Chicago Theological Seminary when a student repeated the Lord's Prayer making just one bold but magnificent change in it. Instead of "Our Father who art in heaven," he said, "Our Father who art in the universe . . . thy will be done on earth as it is in the universe"! Try it, and see what a new shower of meaning falls upon the parched soil of your praying. Yet that is undoubtedly just what Jesus meant.

Heaven to him meant all of the rest of creation which hears God's voice and does his will. We have so associated heaven with golden streets and harps and a great white throne that we need to be brought back to a more realistic theology by a use of language which, while reverent and awe-inspiring, is packed full of contemporary meaning.

Worship and theology, therefore, are inextricably related. To sum it all up we may say, then, first of all, that theology does something for worship. If the theology is poor, the worship will be correspondingly debased. An ancient Babylonian tablet describes how "the gods gathered like flies above the sacrifice" to enjoy its fragrance. Under such a theology worship becomes a means of cajoling and flattering the divine powers. Longfellow has a beautiful poem about Sandalphon, the angel of prayer, based upon a legend in the Jewish Talmud. According to this medieval conception, this angel stands at the gate of heaven receiving the prayers which come up from below and transforming them into the flowers that adorn the heavenly city. This is a much more spiritual and poetical conception than the Babylonian but its effect on worship will be to make it akin to addressing petitions to a far-off king. We have all heard worship services in which this seemed to be the dominant idea. But suppose a theology grips our lives by which we think of God as a present, sustaining and creating Power, a contemporary Force and integrating Intelligence immanent in the universe, with whose thrilling presence we may come into harmony, to whose on-going purpose we may respond? At once worship takes on a depth of emotional feeling, an immediacy and an urgency, which fill it with new significance and earnestness.

On the other hand, if theology can do something for worship, may it not also be true that worship, in its turn, can do something for theology? When people engage in worship they make tremendous assumptions, often hardly realizing how bold and breath-taking these assumptions are. They assume a kinship with God which makes communication with him possible. Much as we may love and be impressed by a planet, a mountain or a tree, we modern men do not pray to these objects of nature. Even the wild animals, beautiful or marvelous as they may be, are alien to us and we learn to recognize and respect the gulf which separates us not only from fierce beings like the tiger or the shark but also from a wood-thrush or a butterfly. Even the animals we have tamed, whether dogs or elephants, still share only very limited and superficial areas of our thought. But God, the soul of the universe, when we worship him, we assume that there are no barriers which cannot be surmounted and that we share with him a direct, complete, perhaps ancestral, understanding as Father, which we hardly have at all with our distant or undeveloped cousins of the animal world. We recognize that we can communicate only with personality akin to our own.

More than this, when we worship we assume an accessibility on the part of God which is real only if there is in the universe something in the nature of mental telepathy or thought transference between our minds and the mind of God akin to that telepathy between our human personalities which we are now trying to explore by scientific tests. What is worship? Just a set of spiritual auto-suggestive setting-up exercises for a man to do faithfully because of their reflex value? Or is it just a tribute of recognition, a kind of high-grade flattery, addressed to God? Or is it the achievement of a cosmic harmony with the ultimate spiritual reality at the heart of all things? If the last conception is ours, and if in the spirit of it we worship, and, as we worship, find that we have actually laid hold of a renewal of courage and strength, of insight, poise and power to endure, then this experience of worship becomes a part of the data with which we must come to terms in the theological wrestle of religion with truth. And, like Jacob of old, we cry out: "I will not let thee go until thou bless me!"

Thus we see that worship is rooted and grounded in theology. It is not just a pleasant exercise for men's spiritual refreshment. It is a tribute which the human soul brings to its Creator, a tribute of awe and wonder, of reverent love, of expressed devotion, of appeal and aspiration. It is not something which is valuable to man alone. We cannot but believe that it has value to God. Having created man, having endowed him with spiritual faculties, surely God must be unsatisfied and disappointed if we never use those faculties to turn to him in spiritual quest and high devotion. Worship is, first of all, something we bring to God, the humble and the contrite heart are still his ancient sacrifice and God still seeketh men to worship him in spirit and in truth. He who conducts public worship, therefore, however much he may hope it will do for those who join with him in its high adventure, must never forget that, first of all and primarily, worship is something done for God. This thought, kept constantly in mind, will give to worship a dignity and beauty, a sense of awe and a spiritual appeal which can come in no other way.

CHAPTER THREE

What Worship May Do for Men

WE READ IN THE GOSPELS concerning Jesus that "as he was praying, the fashion of his countenance was altered." Worship evidently did something for Jesus. What, then, can worship do for men and women today? It may be objected that the worship experiences of Jesus were in the realm of private worship whereas this book deals with public worship. But is not the answer that all public services of worship are first of all personal? It is what goes on in the heart of the individual worshipper that counts. The great value of the public service is that it teaches the individual beautiful and uplifting modes of worship, and that, through the corporate sense of doing things together, it induces a worshipful mood. Also there is often a certain refuge in a crowd, something impersonal that leaves each individual still in the solitude of his own soul. Jesus himself made much use of public as well as private worship. He habitually attended the synagogue and was often in the temple. He went up to the great religious festivals at Jerusalem. He did not abrogate the temple services, he only sought to clear them of graft, confusion and hypocrisy. He sent the lepers whom he cleansed to offer sacrifices and did not advise the man offering his gift before the altar to stop sacrificing, but only to go first and become reconciled to his brother. Evi-

dently public as well as private worship had value for
Jesus. What value may it have for us?

There are, it seems to me, seven great moods or life situations to which worship may minister, namely (1) our need
of common religious fellowship, (2) our sense of spiritual
joy, (3) the quest for deepening insights, (4) the renewal of
faith and vision, (5) our craving for comfort, (6) our need
for confession and absolution and (7) our impulses toward
dedication or re-dedication to God and to our tasks. Let us
look at these values of worship for human lives more carefully and at closer range.

1. *Our Need for Common Religious Fellowship*

Von Ogden Vogt calls attention to worship as being what
he calls the celebration of life. We need not only to live, but
to meditate nobly about living, to objectify life's meaning
and its glory, to consider it in perspective and share our
common hopes and dreams concerning it. All this I take it,
and much more, is involved in the celebration of life. We
are inescapably social beings and a large part of life's
greatest joys are social in their nature. Hence worship needs
to be social. When we get together to pray and sing and
consider about these things, seeing them in the light of
God's will and man's possible greater destiny, we help to
clear the path ahead. Such common worship enlarges our
horizons and quickens our loyalties. Life becomes more
meaningful. One possible origin of the word religion is
that it comes from the Latin verb relegere, which means to
gather together. Religious worship binds us together in the
bundle of the fellowship of worship. When I was a student
at the University of California, troubled with many doubts

over the adjustment of religion, science and modern scholarship, I nevertheless continued to attend church. Each Sunday I saw there Professor William E. Ritter of the zoology department and Professor George M. Stratton, the psychologist, and Professor Thomas R. Bacon, the historian, and Professor Elmer Ellsworth Brown of the department of education. And I knew that in the Episcopal church down the street was Professor Charles M. Gayley of the English department and over at the Presbyterian church, Professor Joseph Le Conte, the great geologist. If religion meant enough for them to attend divine worship, I felt strengthened in my hope that there was something in it for me, too! I was bound with them in the bundle of religious fellowship.

2. *Our Sense of Spiritual Joy*

Early Christian worship with its *agape* or love-feast and its informal spontaneity must have been a much more joyous and even exuberant occasion than it became later when stiffened by too great formality and clouded by the gloom of an over-emphasis on sin, hell, the crucifixion and the blood atonement. The early Christians had no rose-colored view of sin but they did believe, with Paul, that "where sin abounded, grace abounded yet more" and their worship was filled with the joy of a new life in Christ Jesus. Some ministers conduct public worship as if the only people present were mourners or victims of some recent or impending tragedy. To do this is to forget youth, which longs to hear a bugle call to high adventure and see the light on banners in the dawn. It is also to ignore middle age which settles down to the tasks of life rejoicing as a strong man to run a race. It even fails to remember that old age may have a peculiar serenity, like unto Browning's wise old rabbi, and feel that life is good, trusting that the best is yet to be. If worship is to celebrate life, it should celebrate its joy! People should bring not only their sorrows to church but also their shouts of victory. A friend of mine once wrote these lines: [1]

"Still to be sure of the dawn, still to be glad of the sea,
  Still to know fire in the blood—God keep these gifts in me!"

Normal wholesome people feel that way about life. Worship should help them express this joy as an offering to God. Hebrew religion must have been full of this exuberant joy. Read over the Psalms again and see!

Have you never walked along a woodland road uplifted to a new harmony with all that is by the bird-songs in the woods on either side? Have you never felt the sheer joy that cometh in the morning in a mountain meadow or beside the complete stillness of a little lake? Have you never rejoiced with the surge and thunder of the sea? Have you never felt the thrill of long labor to some high purpose, or of hard-earned victory? Have you never found life opening up in new dimensions as you walked the city streets? Have you never rejoiced in the miracle of childhood? All these are moods of great spiritual potentiality and come to their highest when expressed in terms of worship.

3. *The Quest for Deepening Insights*

But no life is just one triumphal march of spiritual joy. Indeed, we could hardly know joy, if we did not also know

[1] Bruce Porter of San Francisco.

uncertainty and struggle. Professor H. N. Wieman has a very valuable section in his little book on *Methods of Private Religious Living* concerning what he calls "worshipful problem solving." The thought of worship as a way to deepening insight opens up values in the church service to which many people are quite blind. Problems are not solved by hard thinking alone. After we have thought as hard and as long about them as we can, we need to commit them to the association paths which exist, we know not how, beneath the level of our normal waking consciousness. To go off and do something else, to take a night's sleep or a week's vacation, may result in a much more balanced view and a wiser judgment. Just here worship may come into a man's life to help him manage his problems.

This help may come in one of two ways. The first is direct. A man takes his problem into the church service and prays about it. Lorado Taft, Chicago's great sculptor, used to experiment with the effect of lights and shadows on statuary. He had casts of great pieces of sculpture in a studio where he could control the lights. One switch sent the light from one side or another, one switch sent it down from above, one up from below. I never shall forget his delight in demonstrating the lighting effects upon Donatello's Boy St. John. When lighted from below the lad looked as though he were little better than an imbecile, but lighted from above he was most adorable! So we may get a new light on our problems, a light from above, as we take them into the worship service and think them through again in the atmosphere of prayer, under the harmonizing influence of great music and against the background of the sonorous wisdom of great passages of scripture. Those who conduct public worship so that it is filled with beauty and nobility may never know what light they are throwing upon unsuspected problems in the minds of members of the congregation.

But there is also an indirect way in which worship may help in solving problems. This is more mysterious but none the less psychologically true. We may not pray about the particular problem at all. Worship may indeed provide the finest sort of a vacation from it. We just come in and lose ourselves in praise and adoration. We allow ourselves for half an hour or so to escape from the world and its troubles and just be upheld by a sense of spiritual serenity and communion. "Oh, rest in the Lord, wait patiently for him," may not be the contralto solo that morning, it may be only your own personal experience. But as a result something happens. The mind clears, the dust of doubt and confusion settles and the storms of passion subside. You have gained a new calm and refreshment through the possession of which you can, in due time, take up your problem with rested nerves and finer insight.

4. *The Renewal of Faith and Vision*

Closely akin to the part worship may play in helping to solve problems is its value in bringing about a renewal of faith and vision. There is a widespread notion that faith and vision are a gift of the gods. They just come to you and you have them or they do not and you do not have them. Some people are particularly fortunate in that they have these outbursts of inspiration and others are just unfortunate in that no such heavenly light is afforded them. Faith and vision are not achieved, they are given. But Paul did not have this idea, he said he had "kept the faith" and kept is an active transitive verb. Ignatius Loyola wrote a famous little book on *Spiritual Exercises*. Worship is one of these spiritual exercises. It lifts our lives out of the merely contemporaneous and brings us into the presence of the greatest hopes and faiths of good men all across the centuries. We are no longer little improvised experimenters. A great worship service renews our fellowship with saints, prophets, martyrs, and we share in an apostolic succession of loyalty to great ideals and spiritual verities.

Nor does worship renew our faith and vision just by reminding us of the past. It actually re-kindles a fire upon the altars of the present. Even as we walk the Emmaus road of our perplexities a presence joins us which opens to us the modern meaning of ancient scripture and turns our faces toward tomorrow. How sad it is that many people go on, week after week, treading a dreary treadmill of fear, discouragement and dull routine when attendance at a worship service might have changed all that. It might, I say, but again it might not! Much depends upon the quality of the worship service for here, again, great responsibility devolves upon the person charged with the conduct of public worship so that, as far as possible, people shall not leave without some quickening of faith and understanding.

5. *Comfort*

People almost instinctively turn to the church and its services for comfort when beaten down or wounded in the battle of life. This may be a positive danger to the public services of the church. They may be made into a kind of anesthetic. Karl Marx's famous objection that "religion is the opiate of the people" should receive careful consideration. Perhaps it is our duty not to make people too comfortable—at least with certain kinds of comfort! "Comfort ye, comfort ye my people, saith your God," according to the fortieth chapter of Isaiah. "Speak ye comfortably to Jerusalem; and cry unto her that warfare is accomplished, that her iniquity is pardoned, that she hath received of the Lord's hands double for all her sins." All very well! But what if it is not to be applied to those whose warfare is not accomplished but who ought still to go on? Or to those whose iniquity needs to be repented of before it can be pardoned? Comfort may be premature!

Nevertheless there are in every congregation those who do stand in need of comfort. Their troubles may have been amply repented of or may be due to no fault of their own. Even so, comfort is not best conceived as an anesthetic, a soothing and lulling to sleep, a running away from reality. The root meaning of the word is *cum*, with, and *fortis*, strength. That service of worship will comfort best which helps people to go back into life and meet their difficulties with strength. Read the rest of the fortieth chapter of Isaiah and it will be evident that the comfort which is to come to Jerusalem arises from a new vision of God who not only carries the lambs in his bosom but who also sitteth above the circle of the earth and bringeth princes to nothing. A sense of the reality and majesty of God is the best comfort and this it is the task of a good worship service to arouse in the discouraged and downhearted.

6. *Confession and Absolution*

If a man do wrong, how shall he again come into right relations with the universe? How can he reestablish peace and harmony with himself, his fellow men and God? If not the greatest of human needs, this is certainly the one of most tragic urgency when it arises. The cry: "I have sinned, I have sinned! What can I do to make things right? How can I ever again be clean and straight and true?"—This cry comes from the bitterest depths of human experience, and the service of public worship must deal with it.

One peril here is that our worship services shall deal with it too lightly: either by omitting it altogether, as though this world were a very refined and cultured utopia where no one ever did wrong; or by repeating the words so easily that they need not be taken too seriously. The prayer of general confession in the English prayer-book is a noble and almost heart-rending cry of penitence, but, when it is hastily read by everybody at the beginning of every morning and evening service, is there not some danger that familiarity may breed contempt or at least complaisancy with the profound contrition which it voices? Would it not be better if such solemn words of spiritual self-searching were uttered as a sort of bidding prayer by the minister, leaving each worshipper to appropriate to his own needs so much of it as comes home to him in his own inner solitude and perfect honesty? And, surely, somewhere in the service there should be a place for a great assurance of pardon for all who "do truly and earnestly repent of their sins and are in love and charity with their neighbors, and intend to lead a new life, following the commandments of God, walking from henceforth in his holy ways." And to no others!

7. Dedication and Re-dedication

Johan Bojer in his appealing novel, *The Great Hunger*,

tells how a man, in spite of a great injury which he had suffered, went out in the year of famine and sowed corn in his neighbor's field "that God might live." God could not live for him and be real and genuine except as he dedicated himself to a generous and even undeserved human service. A friend of mine had carved over the exit doorway of his new church these words in golden letters: "He went about doing good." "It all comes to that at last," he explained to me. "All the praying, all the Bible reading, all the hymn singing, are vain if that isn't the end result." Here then is the ultimate thing that worship can do for man. It can make him want to do good. It has failed completely if it has not created some new sensitivity to the call of God which is ever sounding across creation, "Whom shall I send and who will go for us?" The final response in worship is: "Here am I—with all my weaknesses, inadequacies and even sins, but nevertheless here I am sensitive to human needs and the divine commission—here am I! Send me!"

6280

CHAPTER FOUR

The Historical Background of Christian Worship

To ACHIEVE FREEDOM in the conduct of Christian worship, and also a clearer understanding of its problems, one needs to see it against the background of its history. To know the story of the evolution of the Roman mass or the Anglican prayer-book is to gain a more sympathetic understanding and a new freedom to use the liturgical treasures which these great crystallizations of Christian worship contain. Neither mass nor prayer-book is the peculiar product or property of any one church. They are made up largely of materials coming from an earlier universal Christian tradition and from Jewish and Graeco-Roman elements which are older than Christianity itself. Fortunately none of this material has ever been copyrighted. It is a mine in which we all can dig.

The Christian cultus has two deep roots, one going far down into the Hebrew scriptures and the synagogue and the other into the mystery religions of the Graeco-Roman world. One who knows nothing of the mass, for instance, will at once be struck, and probably surprised, by the large amount of familiar scriptural material, mostly from the psalms, of which it turns out to be composed when read in an English translation. A non-Episcopalian is similarly impressed by the large use made of the psalms in the prayer-book services. It has been asserted that the authors of the prayer-book, being perhaps a little concerned about the disproportionate amount of pre-Christian Old Testament material they were using, sought to Christianize it by prescribing the singing of the gloria with its trinitarian formula after every psalm. If so, they might have Christianized the psalms more effectively by simply omitting certain bloodthirsty passages. At all events that is what we need to do today. To the Christians of the first century, however, "the scriptures" meant the Old Testament, and their earliest worship simply followed Jewish forms of synagogue and family worship plus the emphasis upon Jesus as Messiah and risen Lord, the expectation of his early return, the deeply emotional sense of the Holy Spirit's presence and the feeling of common life which was accentuated by persecution and its perils. As these differences, while highly important from within, were hardly visible from without, it was probably difficult for a pagan observer to distinguish between a Jewish and a Christian synagogue.

One other difference, destined to become distinctive, was the emphasis by Christians on the breaking of bread, the eating of a common meal called the *agape* or love-feast, associated in their minds with the last supper and perhaps with other meals which Jesus had shared with his disciples. How closely Jewish and Christian worship were related, even here however, is revealed by W. E. Oesterley in his book on *The Jewish Background of the Christian Liturgy* where he calls attention to the close resemblance between the accounts of the Lord's Supper and a custom observed by pious Jews of holding a simple preliminary ritual feast of bread and wine before the Passover, at which the following blessings were said:

"Blessed art Thou, O Lord our God, King Eternal,
   Who createst the fruit of the vine," and
"Blessed art Thou, O Lord our God, King Eternal,
   Who bringest forth bread from the earth." [1]

It is interesting to compare this with the instructions given as Christian apostolic teaching in the Didache (c. 90 or 100 A.D.): "As for the eucharist thus must you do it. First, for the chalice: 'We thank thee, our Father, for the holy vine of David thy servant, which thou hast made known to us through Jesus thy servant. Glory to thee forever.' " [2]

But, however Jewish in origin and original phraseology, the Lord's Supper became distinctively Christian in its meaning and the emphasis laid upon it. Although it was a very informal church supper in its earlier form, as described in Paul's protest against the disorderly conduct which had sometimes characterized it at Corinth,[3] it had, nevertheless, a distinctly religious meaning both as a memorial of Jesus and a communion with him. Many features of early Christian worship, the singing, the scripture reading, the prayers, the informal expository talks or exhortations based on scripture, were taken directly over from the synagogue, but the Lord's Supper as a memorial feast was a new and definitely Christian element.

Another Christian addition which has not received so much attention, but which was there from the beginning,

---

[1] W. O. E. Oesterley, *The Jewish Background of the Christian Liturgy*, pp. 79-81 and 167-174.

[2] Percy Dearmer, *Everyman's History of the Prayer Book*, pp. 184-5.

[3] I Cor. 11:20-34.

was the emphasis on ecstatic emotional phenomena supposed to reveal the presence of the Holy Spirit. These included healing and prophesying and, most spectacular of
all, speaking with tongues, which was not a miraculous gift
of foreign languages but highly emotional ejaculations expressive of deep spiritual longings and experience.

These early Christian services must have been very long
and intimate: first a supper together, each family bringing
its own food, as is sometimes done in church suppers today; then a solemn blessing and partaking of the bread
and wine in memory of Jesus; then scripture reading and
prayers and the singing of psalms; then the demonstration
of the presence of the Holy Spirit by a testimony meeting
which included expository and hortatory talks by such as
had the gift of "prophecy," healing or reports of healings,
and ecstatic utterances by those who were emotionally uplifted—the speaking with tongues. Perhaps the nearest approach to this today is found in custom of saying "Amen,"
"Glory to God," "Praise the Lord," "That's right, brother,"
while the minister is praying or preaching which still sur-
vives in certain churches, and in the emotional excitement
of high pressure evangelistic meetings or the still more
ecstatic behavior which characterizes cults like the holy
rollers.

The important, and convincing, thing was that primitive
Christians got results from their religion right then and
there. They did not just go through a ritual as a matter of
duty or in order to insure their soul's salvation after death,
but they actively participated in a series of spiritual exercises out of which they received a thrilling sense of release from sin, of inner power and direct contact with God

which sent them forth ready to face life and even persecution and death with steadfast courage.

But, in addition to the Jewish inheritance from synagogue and scriptures, and in addition to its own distinctive elements like the Lord's Supper, the gift of the Spirit, and emphasis on Jesus and the resurrection, Christian worship was also influenced and enriched by attitudes and possibly even by practices which it absorbed from the mystery religions. Good books are available on these popular cults of the Graeco-Roman world and in this brief sketch we can only pause to point out the influence they probably had on Christian worship. All of them were religions of personal salvation, making large use of instruction, symbolism, drama and personal commitment. Cicero said of the Eleusinian Mysteries, into which he had been initiated, that "they helped men to live more nobly and to die with a fairer hope." Some of them used sacramental meals for communion with their god, some used ceremonial washing, one even practised a baptism in the blood of a bull which was sacrificed on a grating above while the initiate stood beneath drenched in a shower-bath of blood! These mystery religions, good and bad, uplifting or revolting, had grown up in response to human need and they largely set the stage for any religion and established the popular expectations which had to be fulfilled. Communion with some god, deliverance from fear and misfortune, victory over death, fellowship with other believers, characterized all of them to varying degrees. Christianity, when it appeared, must have seemed like just another mystery religion. That it has survived while they have all perished is due, as T. R. Glover has well said, to the fact that Christianity out-thought them, out-lived them and out-died them, which is to say that it had a profounder philosophy, a higher morality and a greater power to endure persecution. The mystery religions, nevertheless, prepared the way for and also deeply influenced the forms of Christian worship, especially in the direction of sacramentalism.

By the time the fourth century had brought freedom from persecution and then made Christianity a state religion, some very notable changes occurred. The services, no longer under necessity of being held in private houses, could now take place publicly in halls designed to hold a large number of worshippers. The old family and church dinner type of service had disappeared and the Lord's Supper had been conventionalized into a sacrament attended by a congregation. The free testimony meeting and exuberant demonstrations of the presence of the Holy Spirit had faded out into proper responses said at proper times by the congregation. There was still a table for the holy supper on the platform, the ministers being seated in the semi-circular apse behind it, but the table itself was completely shrouded in curtains, so sacred had the bread and wine become. The whole service had become a much more orderly and prescribed ritual, though the prayers were still extemporaneous and the congregation had an active sense of participation. About this time outstanding leaders began writing down the ritual they were accustomed to use at the Lord's Supper. One of these, by Serapion, an Egyptian bishop of about 350 A.D., is practically a complete communion service capable of being used almost without change in any protestant church today, except for the intercession in behalf of the souls of the dead.[4]

During the centuries that followed there was a steady crystallization both of dogma and of the forms of worship. By the sixth century the liturgy of the Eastern church was essentially what it is today. In the west, although transubstantiation was not formally proclaimed as a dogma until 1215, the movement in its direction had profoundly influenced church architecture and worship. In the medieval Catholic church the table became an altar, back against the rear wall of the apse. Vestigial reminders of the curtains which had shrouded it in the fourth century still remained in the curtain (dorsal) behind it, and occasionally partial curtains at either side. The minister no longer conducted the service from behind the table and facing the congregation, but now stood as a priest in front of the altar, facing it and with his back to the people. The Lord's Supper, formerly actively participated in by the congregation, had now become the miracle of the mass performed for them by the priest at the altar. The cup was denied to the laity, and the service, as said by the priest in a dead language and largely inaudible to the people, had lost the values of congregational worship which it had in the early church, and had become a formula by which bread and wine are actually changed into the physical body and blood of Christ. The prayers for the dead had become very important since they were the means of rescuing lost souls from purgatory, and a price was exacted for their repetition. On the other hand the service had attained great beauty in color, music and ceremonial and the worshippers

[4] Dearmer, *Everyman's History of the Prayer Book*, pp. 188-191.

had been taught to carry on their own private devotions while the sacrifice of Calvary was being reenacted for them on the altar. The mystery religions had come to their apotheosis in the miracle of the mass! And, correspondingly, the Hebrew element in Christian worship, with its emphasis on instruction, democratic participation and ethical purpose had been submerged in a Graeco-Roman mysticism, while the distinctively Christian elements had been radically transformed. Instead of the active, joyous hope of Jesus' return as Messiah, there was an over-emphasis upon the sufferings of Christ as procuring deliverance from hell in the life to come; instead of a Christ depicted as an almost Apollo-like Good Shepherd carrying a lamb on his shoulders, there was an agonized body hanging on the cross; and instead of the free spontaneous manifestations of possession by the Holy Spirit, there was an inner mystical sense of salvation by the merits of Christ and the bloodless sacrifice of the mass. The service itself had become fixed and changeless in words and ceremonial detail, although there was considerable divergence in different places, the Mozarabic liturgy being prevalent in Spain, the Ambrosian in Milan, the Gallican in France and Ireland, and the Sarum rite, a form of the Gallican, being used in Salisbury Cathedral, England (Sarum is the old name for Salisbury), from whence it spread generally throughout Britain and has partly survived in the English prayer book. But the Roman form of service, most widespread of all, was already on the way to the almost universal dominance which it has today throughout the Roman Catholic world.

Then came the revolutionary upheaval of the protestant

reformation, which, from a liturgical viewpoint, might be interpreted as a revolt against the theological and ceremonial influence of the mystery religions and an attempt to return to a more simple Hebraic conception of Christianity. The reformers, of course, were not intimately acquainted with the mystery religions. They only knew that the Roman form of Christianity, whose corruptions stirred them to rebellion, had a lot of things in it for which they found no warrant in the Bible, and so they sought to purify theology and worship of all things which seemed to them unscriptural and corrupt.

The reformation, obviously, was not a unit. Indeed, one can quite readily classify it into three fairly distinct moods, especially so far as its influence on the forms of public worship is concerned. First, there was the milder type of reformation, as exemplified in the Anglican and Lutheran churches. These movements were thoroughly protestant in theology. They renounced transubstantiation, defied the supreme authority of Rome, dispensed with purgatory, auricular confession, holy water, relics and many ornaments and vestments. But, in the conduct of public worship, they were conservative about making changes. They retained the altar and candles and the pictures in the stained glass windows. The Lutheran minister wore the black scholar's gown and the Anglican came to use, until the Oxford Movement revived more colorful medieval vestments, simply the black cassock, white surplice and stole or scarf. The Bible was given to the people in their own tongue, hymns were sung in the vernacular and the liturgy also was translated into the language the people understood, with such changes as were necessary to make it conform to protestant theology. But the prayers, the responses, the general spirit was much the same as in the earlier Latin service, except that the Lord's Supper became a separate or appended service to the ordinary service of morning prayer.

All this, however, did not go far enough to suit the Puritans. Under the sterner and more relentless reaction of Calvinism much more was done. Go to Holland today and you can still see great medieval cathedrals with all the stained glass broken out and replaced by clear glass and the whole interior whitewashed. The altar was completely eradicated and a plain wooden table placed in the middle of the chancel, the Lord's Supper being celebrated but once a quarter as in Presbyterian churches today. Hating the corruptions of the Roman Church, the Puritan not only dispensed with the old setting of the worship service, he completely changed the service itself, reducing it in stern simplicity to a reading of scripture, singing of psalms, a long prayer and a still longer sermon. Saints' days and Christmas, Lent and Easter, were done away with and even marriage and death were left without religious observance. People were punished at Plymouth for observing Christmas, although eventually it returned. But there are people living who may read this book who can remember when the observance of Easter was a novelty in churches of the puritan tradition. Puritanism was a rebellion against medieval forms of sacerdotalism and the minister, though he wore a black Geneva gown, wore it not because he was a minister but because it was the garb of an educated man.

Even all this was not radical enough for some. When you start a revolution you never know where it will end! And so the protestant reformation had its extremists. These people wanted to do away with everything which did not have literal scriptural command behind it. They proposed to return to the New Testament as they understood it; the Separatists to local church autonomy and the Quakers to utter simplicity in dress and silence in worship, except as moved by the Holy Spirit, for they had rediscovered that long neglected phase in primitive Christian worship.

Now it is easy for modern writers, especially those under the influence of romantic idealizations of medieval life and thought, to speak harshly of the reformers. Doubtless, if we were to meet and talk with them today, we ourselves would find them in some regards very narrow and bigoted. Nevertheless we must be objective enough to see and appreciate what they were after and what they really did accomplish for Christian worship. They proposed to have a thorough house-cleaning of what they felt was idolatry and superstition. The protestant reformers believed in the priesthood of all believers and wanted to protect the laity against a priestly caste. They sought a return to sincerity, directness and intellectual intelligibility. Hence the Bible and the service in the vernacular and the emphasis on the sermon, the hymns sung by all the people and the extemporaneous spontaneous prayer. Even as late as 1930 I heard Principal Selbie of Mansfield College, Oxford, an Oxford Doctor of Divinity, but a free churchman, say in rather peppery mood: "When I hear a Congregational minister begin to read his prayers, I stop praying!" Most of all, these protestant ancestors of ours wanted an inner spirituality, utterly genuine. Hence the discount on elaborate decorations and external things like candles, crucifixes, and other symbols. Their symbol was the clean, bare, undecorated meeting-house, and, in the case of the Quakers, plain gray clothes and silence. These were symbols of deep spiritual integrity and of utter humility before God.

Nevertheless our protestant forefathers, especially the more extreme puritan group among them, lost something. They paid too high a price for what they sought in all sincerity and they did not understand all the needs of human nature. They threw away almost all of the symbols appealing to the eye—lights, color, vestments, pictures, sculpture, even the cross itself in any visible form—and retained the symbols appealing to the ear—Bible reading, preaching, prayer, psalm singing and the creeds. They did this without realizing that these latter things are symbols, too. They also failed to recognize the psychology of clothes! In getting rid of colorful vestments they really only substituted black ones, whether the Geneva gown or the Prince Albert coat, now happily extinct. Even Billy Sunday's shirt sleeves became for him and his followers a kind of vestment! More serious was their loss of architectural values in their stern box-like meeting houses, until Colonial architecture arose to restore grace and beauty to the exterior of the church edifice, at least.

Still more serious were the losses, in Protestantism's extremer manifestations, of great liturgical treasures and traditions which were far older than the corruptions of the medieval church and were founded on permanent psychological values and inescapable human needs. Processions, and lighted candles, chants and responses, beautiful prayers centuries old and a dignified, progressive, truly dramatic order of service—all these were needlessly thrown overboard by the excess of zeal which marked the puritan reformers. And, along with these, went the church year with its orderly and educational procedure, securing variety and preserving historic background. Much glorious music was also lost, in spite of the gains in hymn singing and in the creation of a Protestant musical tradition around the great oratorio of the Messiah. And so, what happened? Human nature came back and demanded some satisfaction for its elemental cravings and so, lacking the steadying guidance of a great tradition, we have our cheap, garish, meaningless church windows, our too ornate and obtrusive organs at the focus of attention, our new sacerdotalism in the over-emphasis on the minister who sits presiding over the congregation as from a throne, our impoverished church music, our improvised orders of worship, our unbowed heads, our conspicuous, whispering, concert-minded choirs, our arm-waving chorus leaders, and our octagonal Akron-plan churches without a restful line, the pews skew-gee to the walls of the building, the overhead beams diagonal to the floor plan, the floor sloping like a theater, and the tower set crosswise to every other dominant line in the whole edifice! And for the church year we have a succession of more or less secular festivals and Sundays for special appeals.

The task of the modern protestant church leader who would rescue Christian worship from the tragic depths into which it has fallen surely now becomes apparent. Understanding the historic development through which Christian architecture, art and liturgy have passed in all the centuries that have gone by, he must feel free to claim and use the best of all the ages. Whatever will minister to human needs and truly interpret the spirit of the Christian message to the world, belongs to us today. "All things are yours, and ye are Christ's and Christ is God's." That text, searchingly applied, is a sufficient mandate for all that needs to be done. As protestants, we are not going to repudiate the essential aims and moral and spiritual values of the reformation. But as, in the noblest use of the word, Catholic Christians, we are free to profit by the whole historic process through which all our spiritual ancestors have gone. All that was good or beautiful in the medieval church belongs to us just as much as to the modern Roman Catholic; and primitive Christianity is even more peculiarly our own because we probably understand its life and spirit better than any of the centuries in between have ever understood that ancient heroic church. Our present task is, therefore, to look at church architecture, at the order of the service and the possible materials of worship with complete freedom. We are to seek to minister to human need for worship with the best and wisest use of all the treasures of architecture, art and literature of all the ages, by no means excluding our own.

CHAPTER FIVE

The Pattern of the Worship Service

As we think of the past, up through which Christian worship has come, questions like these arise in our minds: Might we not well have a variety of services to represent the different Christian centuries and meet different emotional needs and perhaps different types of people today? Is there not a place for extremely simple, intimate group services with a fellowship supper, followed by a simple breaking of the bread in the primitive Christian manner, with scripture readings, informal talks and an intimate exchange of personal experience?

May there not also be a place for the practice of silence and a quiet waiting for the spirit in corporate meditation and inaudible prayer, after the manner of the Friends? But does not human nature also need a fuller and richer use of symbols, the uplifted cross, the candles on the altar, the chanting by a hidden choir, the great forms of prayer where every word is known in advance and comes as an old and familiar friend? On the other hand, if worship is to live, must it not be an adventurous and growing thing? Ought we not, therefore, to encourage experimentations in new forms of worship, and, out of the needs of our own day, prepare fresh litanies of social idealism, and peace, inter-racial brotherhood and economic justice? If modern psychiatric research is giving us deeper insights into prob-

48

lems of the troubled soul and all the tensions and cross currents that make life a turmoil, sometimes below the level of consciousness, must we not seek to create forms of worship which embody this better psychological knowledge and thus minister to minds distraught?

Leaving some of these matters for consideration later on, let us now turn to the Sunday morning service, which is normally the principal worship service of the week in protestant churches. How shall it proceed and what principles can we find to guide us?

It will help to preserve unity and provide a certain psychological pattern for the service if we agree in advance to accept as our basic principle that a worship service should be essentially the recapitulation of a great religious experience. There have been many such. Let us consider some of them.

One of the greatest and most suggestive of all as a pattern for public worship is the beautiful sixth chapter of Isaiah, so effectively used by Dean Sperry and Von Ogden Vogt. Here we have the elements of an ideal worship experience set forth in a clear and psychologically convincing order. First of all there is the sense of need on the part of the worshipper. This experience came to Isaiah "in the year that King Uzziah died." Uzziah's had been a long reign but he died of leprosy, which was a bad omen, and men were dreading what the new administration might do. We, who live in times of political upheaval and uncertainty on a world scale, can easily appreciate Isaiah's apprehensive state of mind as he entered the temple. One of our tasks in conducting morning worship will be to remember the needs which have brought the people into the house of the

Lord. Or, if they are not sufficiently aware of their needs, one function of the sermon, and also of the worship service itself, may be to reveal those needs and stir up a livelier consciousness of them, so that they may return to the Lord's house next time with a clearer sense of the menace of sin and evil.

Once in the temple, Isaiah "saw the Lord sitting upon a throne, high and lifted up." That is to say, he had a vision of God. The vision came to him in terms of his own picture-thinking and scale of values, and we must be careful not to expect to see God through Isaiah's eyes but in terms of our own ideals and highest values. But the important thing is that the people should be helped to see some vision of God and experience some fresh awakening to the presence of the divine in their lives. How this may be accomplished calls for all the consecrated spiritual artistry the leader of public worship can command. Music may well prepare for it—a prelude of quiet and peace, which shall bring a sense of harmony beyond our jangled daily lives. Absolute cleanliness and quiet reverence in the place of worship, a dim religious light, some great symbol of our Christian faith at the focus of attention such as a cross or a great open Bible and two candles burning on the communion table may all help. The words of some sonorous scripture passage from the prophets or the Psalms, read with great dignity and quiet assurance, may convey to the worshipper a feeling that this is indeed the house of God and the gate of heaven. Most important of all may be the invocation, in which brief prayer the minister lifts all the congregation to a sense that God is here seeking men to worship him in spirit and in truth. However it is done, it is tremendously important that there be no false motions, nothing trivial or improvised, at the opening of the worship service but that the people come to feel at once that they are being called to a great experience and want to be hushed and expectant, as before the gates of some great temple.

Following Isaiah's worship experience as a pattern, the next thing that happened was a deep feeling of unworthiness and contrition on Isaiah's part. This humility and repentance was both individual and social. "Woe is me! for I am undone; because I am a man of unclean lips, and I dwell in the midst of a people of unclean lips: for mine eyes have seen the king, the Lord of Hosts." Humility, contrition, a sense of sin, come when our petty pride is broken down and put in proper perspective by the contemplation of purity, truth and beauty. How to present the greatness of the spiritual ideal so that people will reach out toward it and, in doing so, pour contempt on all their pride, is part of the task of a leader in public worship. This may come through great music, great scripture, noble and uplifting prayers and soul-searching, tremendously sincere, preaching. Let no one say: "But the time has not yet come in the order of service for the sermon!" True as that may be of a single service, the function of the sermon is so to stir the heart and conscience of the worshippers that it shall prepare them for the next worship service and the next. It should create a mood and a grasp of spiritual things which will project itself into all the worship experiences of the future.

But it is not enough to awaken the mood of confession and penitence. Relief and comfort, cleansing and forgiveness, must also be provided. Something in the service should take a coal from off the altar and cleanse the worshipper with purifying power until he knows that his iniquity is taken away and his sin forgiven. What should happen now? Surely a new sensitivity to the voice of God, a greater readiness to hear the call that comes from the source of all ideals and holy purposes, "Whom shall I send, and who will go for us?" If the worshipper now can answer, "Here am I, send me!" the great object of dedication has been attained. What then remains is to reinforce and strengthen the new-born purpose to meet the hardships, the postponements and defeats, which await even the most completely consecrated soul in a wicked world. Here the sermon and even the benediction may play an important part.

Isaiah's vision is, however, not the only pattern to guide us in planning a worship service. The Lord's Prayer may well be studied in this connection. Into a few brief words Jesus has here condensed a whole philosophy of religion. It is a veritable epitome of his teaching, it is Christianity in miniature! Try to fashion a worship service upon it and see what happens! First of all, as in Isaiah's case, the sense of need. The Lord's Prayer was given in response to a request: "Lord teach us to pray!" Always the minister has the problem on his soul of how to stir people out of their imprisoning complacency and make them realize their need of something greater than their own self-satisfied contentment with themselves and the status quo. Then comes, again as in Isaiah, the uplifted and uplifting sense of God. "Our Father who art in heaven" or, to modernize it, "Our Father who creates and sustains the universe, the living wisdom and unseen power within the cosmic order." The effect of this is to lift one above petty concerns and worries. The worshipper moves into a grander atmosphere and has concern for greater issues. He waits in reverence before a spiritual presence, "Hallowed be thy name," and forgets his individual needs in the imperial objectives of God himself: "Thy kingdom come, thy will be done on earth as it is in heaven." All this might well be expressed in the first great movement of a noble worship service.

But now the mood of the service changes. Following the on-going movement of the prayer the service comes down to earth. "Give us this day our daily bread," suggests the economic needs and concerns of all of us. Note, as Walter Rauschenbusch has pointed out, the plural with all its social implications. Here is the place for a litany of industrial ideals. All of man's labor and his control of the labor of others, by which daily bread is brought to the human race, may well come into the thought of the worshipping congregation. I know a little boy who says this grace at table:

"We thank thee, Father, kind and good,
For all who work to give us food."

There you have an ideal for a worship service, an ideal which, if some of our great industrial leaders could have absorbed it in childhood, or could yet absorb it as they bow in childlike humility before God's presence, might help solve the problems of labor and the bitterness of industrial strife.

The next high thought in the service will be "Forgive us our trespasses as we forgive those who trespass against us." Right personal relations, the harboring of no grudges,

the effort to see and understand the other person's viewpoint, the permanent attitude of forgiveness and good will:
how much humanity needs all this! And, as James Gordon
Gilkey has suggested, forgiveness needs to be stretched so
that we forgive life and the universe as well as persons. To
cherish no resentments against life itself, no bitterness over
what might have been—this, for many a troubled soul,
would be the best forgiveness of all. There is a mood to in-
culcate in morning worship which, if it could be seen and
accepted, might transform people who entered the church
this morning with frowns on their faces and bitter scowls
in their memories!

But the service is not ended yet. "Lead us not into temp-
tation, but deliver us from evil," strikes a still deeper note.
It is, like the "Let me never be confounded" at the end of
the Te Deum, a plea for personal integrity, a longing that
life may continue whole and steady, unbroken by trials
and unstained by corroding sin. "And having done all, to
stand!" is the ultimate deep prayer of the soul, to be at
last undefeated in the inner citadel of one's own life! One
can close the service now in the spirit of the final ascription, "For thine is the kingdom and the power and the
glory, forever. Amen." This again brings the worshipping
congregation back to the opening mood, links life up to God
and undergirds it with his grace and power.

It might also help to think of a worship service as a
pilgrimage. Like Bunyan's immortal drama of the inner
life in Pilgrim's Progress, it begins with the realization of
a burden and that one dwells in the City of Destruction.
The Slough of Despond is hard by and the blandishments
of Mr. Worldly Wiseman. Here again, you see, worship

springs from the sense of need. The function of the service, then, is to point out the wicket gate or conduct the congregation through the Interpreter's House until at the foot of the cross the burden slips away. Another service may begin on the Hill Difficulty, meet and recognize the lions in the way and lead to the Palace Beautiful. And so one may go on, for Bunyan knew the principles of alternation and ascension in his pilgrimage. The Palace Beautiful is succeeded by the battle with Apollyon and the cage in Vanity Fair, but beyond are the shepherds in the Delectable Mountains and the Eternal City. The skillful leader of worship will minister to these different moods, meeting them in alternating rhythm but always ascending higher into the mountain of the Lord.

Yet another admirable pattern for a worship service which shall have unity and yet a progressive unfoldment is to be found in St. Francis de Sales' *Introduction to a Devout Life*. This has been simplified and condensed by Ozora Davis for use in the Thorndike Hilton Chapel of The Chicago Theological Seminary and while, in its present form, it is designed for guidance in personal meditation, the skillful builder of a service of worship will recognize at once how adaptable it would be as a pattern for public as well as private devotions.

First Step—Preparation

Let the imagination be active.

Place yourself in the presence of God.

Affirm that since God is everywhere, He is now here; and you are in the very atmosphere of His nearness, like a flying bird in the air.

Think of Christ, "whom not having seen ye love," as now in

this Chapel sharing your experience, although unseen, as once He lived with men.

Offer a brief prayer of confession and petition, imploring guidance in the moments of meditation to follow.

Propose a subject, making it as specific and vivid as possible. Imagine it as connected with some definite action or part of your experience.

Second Step—Consideration

Let the mental powers be active.

Entertain all possible considerations of the subject proposed, in order to make it clear and convincing to the mind. Seek solid reasons for the proposition, assured that the religious life may be based on facts and logical conclusions.

Go from point to point in the consideration without hurry or fatigue. Proceed only so far as time and a composed mind will permit.

Third Step—Resolution

Let the feelings and the will be active.

The reasons reached in the consideration should stimulate the affections, since we must love better what is more fully known.

Reduce general considerations, thus warmed by the emotions, to the form of definite duties to be presented to the will for acceptance.

Resolve firmly and reverently, "I will now undertake to build my life upon that which I have considered and which has been clarified in my meditation."

Fourth Step—Conclusion

Offer a prayer of thanksgiving for the new truth discerned and the new resolution registered.

Offer a prayer of consecration to the practical duties and the enlarged life involved in the resolution.

Offer a prayer for grace and strength to keep steadfastly in the way of duty until the resolution is fully carried out.

Then, as one who has been walking in a garden of flowers gathers a few to take with him, select a truth or an impression and carry it in memory for the day.
"And the peace of God, which passeth all understanding,
    shall guard your hearts and your thoughts in Christ Jesus."

Looking back over this chapter one realizes that the principle of organizing a worship service around some great experience of religion affords not only a sound psychological procedure but also a possibility of wonderful variety. And yet some things are constant: the sense of God's presence, the attitude of humble confession and need of forgiveness, the alternation and ascension of moods, the elevation above personal and worldly troubles, a temporary escape from them, indeed—on the one hand—and a renewed dedication, an acceptance of life and courageous facing of its problems—on the other. These things in balance and developing expression make up the pattern of the worship service.

To make all that has gone before much more concrete and definite, let us now work out an order for the Sunday morning service along the lines which have been indicated. This is by no means a perfect or final or definitive order of worship, but it at least will serve to illustrate the direction in which the considerations already given will lead us.

ORDER OF MORNING WORSHIP

(Note: The service will proceed without announcement of the several parts.)

Organ Prelude.

(This would establish an atmosphere of worship. It should, therefore, be meditative and quiet rather than noisy. Before it begins the church should, of course, be immaculately clean, quiet and in perfect order. While it is being played a boy in choir robes may come in with a taper and light the candles on the communion table. No scratching of matches should be permitted.)

Call to Worship.

(As the organ prelude softens to a close, the voice of the minister is heard in the distance as he makes an opening prayer for and with the choir, to which the choir responds with an Amen or brief musical response.)

Processional Hymn.

(During which the choir marches in, followed by the minister, the congregation rising and remaining standing until after the Invocation and Lord's Prayer.)

Scripture Sentences and Invocation and Lord's Prayer.

(Said by the minister from the lectern. Sentences such as "God is a Spirit and they that worship him must worship him in Spirit and in truth" or "I was glad when they said unto me: Let us go unto the house of the Lord"; or "Praise waiteth for thee, O God, in Zion, and unto thee shall the vow be performed." These sentences, and the brief invocation which follows them, should be changed from month to month so that they may not become routine and monotonous.

Anthem.

(Striking the note of praise and faith in God.)

Scripture Lesson.

(Not necessarily the passage which contains the text of the morning's sermon, but some great, uplifting portion of Holy Scripture calculated to awaken the reverence and spiritual aspirations of the congregation.)

Hymn.

(Carrying on and enabling the congregation to express the mood of the Scripture lesson. Congregation standing.)

Confession of Faith.

(The congregation remains standing for this and the Gloria

which follows. Different confessions of faith may be used in rotation through the year.)

Gloria Patri.

Call to Prayer:

(Read responsively, the people kneeling or seated with bowed heads. This call should be changed at least monthly, but the following will illustrate what is meant.)

M. God is a Spirit, and they that worship him must worship him in spirit and in truth.

P. O come let us worship and bow down, let us kneel before the Lord our maker.

M. God is Light, and the Father of Lights in whom is no variableness neither shadow that is cast by turning.

P. O Lord, send out thy light and thy truth, let them lead us to thy holy hill.

M. God is Love, and he that dwelleth in love dwelleth in God and God in him.

P. O Thou who makest the outgoings of the morning and evening to rejoice, keep us in thy love this day and forevermore.

Choir Response: "Bless the Lord, Oh my Soul."

Period of Silent Worship.

The Pastoral Prayer, followed by Choral or Organ Response.

(This prayer should sound the notes of Thanksgiving, Awe, Penitence, Faith, Petition, Communion. As the whole range of religious need and aspiration cannot be traversed any one Sunday, the minister will do well to keep some sort of record and plan of his pastoral prayers that he may not travel in too narrow a groove.)

Hymn (In devotional mood, following the prayer.)

Announcements, if any are necessary.

Sermon:

(Followed by a brief prayer of dedication and committal, if the minister feels moved to do so.)

Choir Response.

Offertory.

Sentences by the minister: ("Ye remember the words of our Lord Jesus, how he said that it is more blessed to give than to receive," or other appropriate verses.)

Taking of the offering and bringing it to the chancel.

· Service of dedication of the gifts and of ourselves. (By choir chant, or doxology or brief responsive reading, followed by prayer of dedication.)

Recessional Hymn. (A hymn of Christian purpose and consecration, the choir alone singing the last stanza, outside, a capella.)

Benediction. (Followed by chanted amen by the choir outside.)

Postlude. (In keeping with the spirit of the service. Postludes often tend to be too loud and blatant!)

If desired the sermon can, of course, be placed after the offertory. There are gains and losses in both arrangements. In a small church it may be well to omit the processional and recessional and begin with the call to worship from the pulpit. Even a very limited choir in a very small church, however, can learn to sing responses which will add much to the emotional feeling and continuity of the service, using single verses of old and familiar hymns for this purpose. In other churches, if time permits, additional music or a responsive scripture reading or a reading from extra-Biblical sources may well be added. A litany or responsive prayer may precede the pastoral prayer, particularly when the hymn book contains such worship material properly designated by a reference number so that it can be indicated on the printed or mimeographed order of service as easily as a hymn. Unfortunately many hymn book editors have never awakened to the importance of such reference numbers.

CHAPTER SIX

The Architectural Setting

ROMANESQUE, BYZANTINE, Renaissance, Mission, Georgian, Colonial, Classical, Gothic, Modernistic—in which style of architecture should a Christian church be built? Let us recognize right at the beginning that beautiful churches have been built in all these styles, and will continue to be. There is no one "Christian" architecture. In the orient we shall doubtless even see Christianity finally quite at home in buildings with the curved tile roofs and broad-spreading eaves of a Buddhist temple or Shinto shrine. At the same time we must recognize that all of these styles can be so parodied or perverted or so unintelligently used that their value for spiritual aspiration is largely lost. The principles that underlie the architectural setting of Christian worship are, then, deeper and more fundamental than any particular architectural pattern but apply to every style alike. They are the conditions to which all architecture must conform if it is to serve the high cause of Christian worship. It is, therefore, not as a "classicist" or a "gothicist" or a "modernist" that one must approach problems of architectural setting but as a "liturgist." Christianity is not an architectural partisan. It grew up in the open courts of Graeco-Roman private houses. It found the Roman law-court or basilica to its liking in the fourth century. It developed the Romanesque, which evolved into medieval

Gothic under influences which were a fascinating combination of theological ideas, liturgical changes and structural adventure. It found, in other centuries and other moods, a home in the baroque, the Spanish mission, the Georgian, the Colonial. And now, as we move out into structural steel and glass and plain walls, without cornices or windows, be assured that the spirit of Christian worship will find expression in this modern style, too; as, indeed, it already has, notably in German and Scandinavian countries.

But, whatever the style chosen, the liturgical requirements which underlie good church architecture remain permanent and inescapable. This is because they are based on essentially psychological principles and the human mind is still the human mind whatever school of architecture surrounds it. If it is a good, unprejudiced, truly cultured human mind it will enjoy many architectural forms; but it will, at the same time, require of them all certain basic virtues. Stability, unity, harmony, integrity, repose, correlation of structural form and functional purpose, appropriateness to use and environment, are some of the fundamental tests to which all architecture, past, present or yet-to-be, must inevitably be subjected. In the same way there are underlying conditions necessary to the effective conduct of public worship which apply equally to them all. This ought to be a comforting thought to those who probably never will have an opportunity to build their "dream church" in some favorite style but are, of necessity, bound to accept some edifice inherited from the past and try to make it more adaptable to the purposes of Christian worship.

Of course there are church buildings which are almost

hopelessly bad. This is because they are true to no one great school of architecture but are merely unintelligent imitations or stupid mixtures in defiance of all sound principles. In some such cases the only helpful advice that can be given is an earnest entreaty to keep the building well insured! But, even in church buildings which are far from good, a careful observance of sound principles as to the architectural setting for worship can go a long way in overcoming the handicap of nondescript or even bad design. How much can be done against great odds, and yet at modest cost and by simple means, has been well illustrated by a Congregational minister in Wisconsin. He had for a church only the square gaunt room of a town hall, used ordinarily for shows and dances and political meetings. But on Sundays he transformed it into what was undeniably a shrine for Christian worship, and he did so by the simplest means. As a background he placed a screen of fir boughs from the woods near by. In front of that an old table, rescued from a scrap-heap and made strong and massive by some slabs of Norway pine from a neighboring wood-pile. On the table he placed a home-made cross of beautiful white birch—also growing in the adjacent woods—and on one side of the table the simplest possible lectern, also of white birch, while on the other side a few fir boughs made a choir rail and screen for the little cottage organ. It only took brains and taste, a little work and almost no money whatever!

Now what are the principles to be observed in order to secure an effective setting for a service of Christian worship? First let us think of the exterior and its surroundings and then of the arrangement of the interior.

THE EXTERIOR

The exterior of a church should say to the passer-by: "This is a place of Christian worship. It is loved and honored by the people who attend it; and it is hospitable and friendly, with a warm welcome for all who enter." How can all this be translated into architecture? In many ways! The size and shape of the lot, and the location of the church upon it, are important items, to begin with. Too many American churches are built in stark and relentless fashion right up to the property line. Nothing intervenes between them and the harsh and noisy city street. When I was in Japan I was much impressed with the natural beauty with which temples in that country always are surrounded. You do not step right off the street into a Shinto or Buddhist temple but, first of all, you pass through a garden along a winding path and under noble trees. Only after nature has had a chance to bathe your soul in beauty do you approach the shrine itself. Of course such a setting is not always possible in crowded American urban conditions, but it is possible for suburban and rural churches; and, even in the city, if it were held as an ideal it could be realized far more frequently than you may believe. Central Union Church in Honolulu, for example, moving out of the crowded business section, purchased an old eight-acre estate, in the midst of which it built what was lovingly called "the church in a garden;" and here and there in America one finds a suburban church which has discovered the beauty of nature as an appropriate vestibule to the worship of God.

But, even if an adequate landscape setting is not possible,

much can be done to make the exterior say the things it ought to say to the passer-by and possible comer-in. A tasteful hedge or narrow garden bed in place of weeds, some shrubbery or tall slender trees to soften the bare and sometimes too angular structure of the building, say a great deal as to the love and regard in which people hold their church. Paint and cleanliness say something, too! If the building is not in very good style the painting can help minimize ugly lines by using solid color throughout instead of accenting the window casings or other supposedly decorative mouldings. Even an edifice otherwise unattractive wins the respect of the passer-by if, at least, it is clean and well painted, with no loose boards or broken windows, and the yard landscaped and well cared for.

Should the building have a sign or bulletin board? By all means, for this is a very definite expression of welcome and of interest in the newcomer and the stranger. But it should not be a secular or commercialized type of sign. I remember a lovely little church in Oakland, California, set far back from the street and approached by a walk along a narrow strip of garden. Where this walk joined the street there was an attractive little lich-gate, roofed over so that one could rest in its shade and with a projecting arm carrying the name of the church on a swinging sign. Above the roofed gateway was a simple wooden cross. The whole thing indicated unmistakably the entrance to a church and added a touch of beauty and hospitality which was most attractive. That church was fortunate in having a real artist on its board of trustees! Whatever sign or lighted bulletin board is used should be distinctly ecclesiastical in design and, if possible, framed in trees and shrubbery. And, speaking of lights, there is no reason why the entrance to a church should be dark and gloomy so that people stumble about trying to find their way in at night. Indeed, a properly lighted doorway may be a real symbol of religion. "I am the door," said Jesus, "I am the light of the world. He that followeth me shall not walk in darkness."

INTERIOR

As a setting for worship, however, the interior of the church is vastly more important than the exterior. In this book we are dealing with adaptation to public worship only and not with the whole field of church architecture and so no consideration will be given to the necessity of equipment for religious education and church social work, important and valuable as these activities are, but only to the planning of a church interior most fitting and helpful to Christian worship.

One basic consideration is that the place of public worship, whether it be called the auditorium or the sanctuary or simply the church, be neither too large nor too small for the normal congregation. But, because congregations vary widely at different seasons of the year and with the ebb and flow of population, this means that a church auditorium should be planned with the idea of taking care of unusually large congregations on special occasions and also, and perhaps even more important, of serving smaller congregations without making them feel lost or lonesome in too vast an edifice. This can be done in a number of ways.

In a large church the chancel, if there is one, may be used as a place for small meetings, thus providing an in-

American Seating Co. photo.

St. Lucas Evangelical Church, Evansville, Indiana, before
and after remodelling

timate friendly grouping in the presence of the rich religious symbolism of the chancel itself. Many a large
church is now being equipped with a small chapel, also,
seating from fifty to a hundred and fifty people, arranged
with such beauty and religious symbolism that it becomes
a shrine for private devotions, and a cherished place for
weddings, christenings, funerals and small group devotional services. Such a chapel should be readily accessible
to the street, so that it may be left open at all times, even
when the church is closed, as an invitation to all who pass
its door to enter, rest and pray. If some kind of a light is
always burning it will help to keep such a shrine from
seeming empty and have the added incidental value of
guarding it from the vandalism of the heedless or the ignorant. A light, somehow, makes it "come alive," and says
to the worshipper, and even to the intruder: "This is a place
where people love to come. It is not empty and deserted.
God is here, and his children come here, too!"

But, where no such smaller chapel is available and one
church room must accommodate all services, much can still
be done to make it adjustable to congregations of varying
sizes. One reason for preferring a relatively long narrow
church is that, by the simple expedient of laying heavy
cords across the entrances to the pews at the back of the
church, a smaller congregation, say in summer, can be concentrated in the front. A balcony in the rear extending back
over the vestibule may be quite unused and ordinarily forgotten and yet provide available space for several hundred more on special occasions. Similarly a transept and
transept galleries can be so arranged that they are there,
even curtained off, ready for use when needed but not

at all conspicuous. Indeed the ordinary congregation filling the nave will hardly be conscious of them at all. Thus
a church may seat, say, three hundred in the nave, a hundred more in the back balcony, a hundred more in each
transept and so serve a maximum congregation of six hundred; or a normal congregation of three hundred; and still
not seem empty, if only one hundred are present but concentrated in the front pews. How important this is anyone
will recognize who has ever conducted a service with one
hundred participants scattered all over a vast empty square
box planned to seat from six hundred to a thousand! Yet
another device is to seat the church with light chairs easily
moved and rearranged, placing on the floor at each service
only the number likely to be required and spacing them
accordingly. Thus the church always seems relatively full,
whatever the size of the congregation. The fellowship values of worship are, of course, greatly handicapped by a vast
area of empty pews and correspondingly enhanced if practically every seat is occupied.

Another reason for preferring a relatively long and narrow nave to a church which is square or octagonal or
broader than it is long lies in the fact that the seats can
fill the entire nave, except for the middle aisle, while the
side aisles can be replaced by an ambulatory along the
nave on either side and opening into it by broad archways.
The succession of these arches on either side has distinct
psychological value in leading the mind on toward the chancel while the long narrow proportions of the nave give a
pleasing sense of depth even in a small building. This is accentuated by the aisle in the middle leading on into the chancel, by the arrangement of the chancel itself, especially if

there is a curtain at the end of the chancel behind the communion table. This is pleasing because it does not stop the eye or put up barriers at any point but says to the mind of the worshipper in the pew: "There is progress here! Life goes on! There is more beyond, even beyond the furthermost wall of the church!" This is why a window, if the light through it be soft rather than glaring, is so welcome at the end of the chancel above the altar or communion table. One rustic chapel in Wyoming frames the peaks of the Grand Tetons in such a window and the chapel at Asilomar in California lets you look out on the sand dunes and glorious old live oaks. But a church of which I was once pastor in a crowded city got the same effect by filling the end of the chancel wall with a great landscape painting, mostly fleecy white clouds in a blue sky, with low rounded hills and close-clinging trees below. It reminded every worshipper that the whole earth is full of His glory and that, on beyond our little human walls and the noisy city street, there still exist the wonder, peace and beauty of the out-of-doors.

Supposing, then, that we agree that our church room should preferably be long and narrow, with an ambulatory along each side. Then how high should it be? High enough to give adequate cubic air contents, high enough so that the congregation does not feel conscious of the ceiling, which had better be left in shadow rather than conspicuously illuminated. And the floor should be level, not bowled or sloping. In a theater both the bowled floor and slightly sloping stage may help the audience see all the action in a play but in a church the only points they need to see, which are the pulpit, the lectern and the communion table, can easily be made visible by placing them at proper elevations, while the preservation of a level floor gives much better proportions to the room and avoids making the ambulatory arches increasingly low and squatty toward the rear of the room. Moreover, a church built like a theater involves setting up in people's minds the associations of a theater, whereas a church should establish an atmosphere of its own.

Lighting the church deserves special study, as has been emphasized by Professor Eastman in a recent article.[1] In the daytime the "dim religious light" can certainly be overdone, for while a church should not be so bright and glaring that there are no shadows and no sense of mystery, neither should it be dark, gloomy and depressing. Stained glass windows, especially those with poorly drawn figures, raw colors or intricate and meaningless geometrical designs have been the bane of American church architecture for the last fifty years. I once had a church which had such a curious pattern in the windows that someone dubbed it "the church of the holy cuttle-fish"! Once you had seen those two eyes and encircling tentacles in almost every window, you could never quite forget them! I would, therefore, plead for plain glass as against most arbitrary conventional designs. Where there are lovely trees outside, plain glass can be used; or, if the outside landscape is not attractive, a rough amber cathedral glass in small leaded panes. Or, if great economy is necessary, the cheapest glass obtainable can be used and simply painted some soft harmonious

[1] *Relight Your Church*, by Prof. Fred Eastman. "Chicago Theological Seminary Register," Vol. 27 No. 4 Nov., 1937. Also printed in "The Christian Herald."

translucent color. Of course really beautiful stained glass of genuine artistic quality is always desirable but it is better to have none at all than to suffer from cheap glass of poor design and harsh colors.

When it comes to electric lights, the church has much to learn. There are five fundamental principles which should guide the electric lighting of church interiors.

1. No exposed lights in view of the congregation. Many people suffer unpleasant eye-strain and others are put to sleep by the piercing glare of little spots of electric light in the direct range of their vision. All lighting should be indirect or semi-indirect and from concealed sources.

2. It is desirable that certain parts of the building should be more luminous than others, notably the pulpit, lectern, communion table and choir, but this can easily be accomplished by flood lights so placed that the congregation is quite unconscious of them.

3. The volume of light should be capable of regulation by a system of rheostat control so that it can be made brighter or softer, as the mood of the service may suggest, brighter for the singing of the hymns or any part where the congregation needs to see to read, and softer during the prayer or the sermon.

4. The control of the light should be concentrated at some strategic point, probably best, as Professor Eastman has suggested, at a switchboard beside the organ so that the organist can do the regulating.

5. Simplicity and economy as to fixtures. Fixture manufacturers are of course, eager to design elaborate and expensive brackets and chandeliers. These often become too prominent, calling attention to themselves, whereas simple,

unobtrusive and much less expensive designs would have been preferable.

A few prosaic words need to be said at this point about the pews! They need not be uncomfortable! If they are, it is because they are too narrow, or have backs that are too low or too upright or not upright enough, or because they are crowded too close together. A good seating company ought to have correct cross-sections and dimensions, but if you build your own, build a few samples first and have different people try sitting in them for a whole hour, not just a few minutes. Pews are terribly permanent and a mistake in their design may handicap the effectiveness of worship services for years to come. They should, of course, be equipped with racks for books, cards and pencils and holders for individual communion cups, except in churches where the people receive communion at the altar rail. The communion cup-holders should have felt on them to make them noiseless. Hats and overcoats clutter up pews and this could be avoided if the church would provide a convenient checkroom adjacent to the vestibule. But the most important thing about pews seems hopeless of accomplishment, short of the millennium, and that is to get the first comers to take the end away from the aisle so that those who come later need not scramble over them. There is a name for people who sit down resolutely in the end nearest the aisle but it is too impolite to be included in this book!

CHANCEL

How shall we arrange the part of the church where the choir and minister lead in the conduct of the service? In the old colonial churches of New England the choir and sometimes an orchestra were located in a gallery in the rear above the entrance vestibule while the minister occupied a monumental pulpit in front—sometimes a two- or three-decker. This happy arrangement went out of style in the nineteenth century, though it has strong points in its favor and might well be revived, especially in churches of colonial design. It leaves the choir in an inconspicuous position and there is much wisdom in the motto that choirs, unlike children, should be heard and not seen. At the University of Chicago, in its vast cathedral-like chapel, there are two choirs: one which marches in the processional, sits in the chancel and leads the congregational singing; and another, high up in a second balcony at the extreme rear of the chapel, which, unseen of men, produces heavenly music which floats down upon the congregation.

The worst of all arrangements for the pulpit end of the church, and by far the most common, is to have the choir directly back of and above the minister with towering organ pipes behind and above the choir, and the organist perched on a high bench in view of everybody. This arrangement is bad for the minister because he has to preach with all the choir members for a background. If one of them yawns, or goes to sleep or whispers or passes a note, the whole congregation sees it and is correspondingly distracted. No choir can give one hundred per cent attention all the time, especially to a speaker whose face they cannot see. Besides, some of them may have been out late at a party the night before! And then, too, the minister may not be one hundred per cent interesting! Every public speaker would prefer a plain wall or a soft curtain for a background rather than even the most perfectly disciplined choir in Christendom.

Moreover, this arrangement is almost equally bad for the choristers because it almost inevitably suggests and creates the concert psychology. They cannot help but feel that they are up there to sing to the congregation, especially to the music committee, and perhaps also to Mrs. Millions or to the president of the Zenithville Womans Club or to the Professor of the Music School. No applause is customary, but a discerning choir easily recognizes when it has made a hit with these and other important people in the audience. Now all this does not contribute to the worship value of the morning service, rather it hinders it, especially if the conductor directs the choir with calisthenic enthusiasm from a high stand. A concert is, or may be, a delightful secular occasion but it is not a service of worship, and the singing of religious or at least theological words, does not make it so if the mental attitudes and physical setting of a concert still remain. Music in the church service ought to be rendered to the Lord, as St. Paul advised, and not to men. The choir is present, not to sing to the congregation, but to lead them in their worship. How can this be accomplished?

Before we attempt to answer this question, let us raise another. What shall be done with the communion table? In the typical arrangement, with a central pulpit and the choir in serried rows above and behind it, the communion table is placed inconspicuously on the floor of the church below the pulpit, if indeed it is not omitted altogether. If the church is also used for the Sunday-school assembly, it tends to become the repository for the superintendent's call-bell, extra quarterlies, notes and memoranda, class-books, collection baskets and the birthday bank. These may be removed before the church service—or they may not. If

they are, two piles of empty offertory plates take their
place. In any case the tendency is to minimize the symboli-
cal value of the table, in spite of the carved words, "In
Remembrance of Me," which probably adorn its front. The
table may be relatively insignificant in size, sometimes a
mere stand, and anyhow it is too conveniently located for
too many other purposes to have any outstanding significance as a reminder of the last supper of Jesus and his
disciples. Along with the overcoming of the concert psychology on the part of the choir we, therefore, have this
added problem: how to restore the communion table to a
place of dignity and reverence where its value as a symbol
of the Lord's Supper can be safeguarded and emphasized.

One more problem is involved. It has to do with the
over-conspicuousness of the minister in the ordinary arrangement described above. He is, to be sure, sometimes
completely hidden by a cavernous pulpit, up above which
he appears at intervals like a jack-in-the-box. But, as pul-
pits diminish in size he is more often located in one of
three big chairs sitting alone in front of the choir rail. All
eyes in the congregation see him. There is no escape for
him. There he is, perched up like a city set on a hill. With
the passing of the years he may become callous to this en-
forced exhibitionism; but, after all, is it necessary or desirable? Is it good for him to be so conspicuous and seem
to be presiding over the congregation when, in reality, he
ought to be leading them in an experience of worship?
Would not the truly humble and modest minister prefer a
less exalted seat when not actually called upon to take a
leading part in the ritual? This problem also needs to be

considered along with those of the location of the choir and the communion table.

The best answer to all three difficulties seems to be the chancel type of arrangement. The Episcopalians and Lutherans have largely led in this but its use is increasing rapidly among Presbyterians, Congregationalists, Methodists, Baptists, Disciples and other denominations. The Roman Catholics use it in modified form, placing the choir in a rear gallery as did the old New England puritans.

The advantages of the chancel arrangement are obvious. First of all, the communion table is central. It may become, in churches which desire it, an altar back against the end of the church with a reredos or, probably better still, a curtain behind it. In churches practicing baptism by immersion, this has the advantage of also giving a central position to the baptistry which can be located behind this curtain, the curtain being drawn apart when the baptistry is used. But other churches will recognize that the communion table, as a table, is an older, simpler and, for them, a preferable symbol; and so, instead of an altar, they will prefer a simple but massive table, well back in the chancel but with a bench behind it on which the minister may sit during the communion service. At other times the table may be covered by a deep red or crimson velvet cloth, and on it may be placed two candles and a slender well-proportioned cross. Or, if local sentiment does not welcome a cross, rather than make the cross a cause of contention, a great open Bible on an inclined reading stand may be placed between the candles, or a large bouquet of flowers. Or a seven-branched candlestick may fittingly occupy the center of the table. All are symbols of spiritual values and serve both to exalt and dignify the table and also to place at the focal point of the church some object which conveys a spiritual message to everyone who enters it.

In such a chancel the choir will face toward the center of the church, forming two sides of a hollow square or oblong, of which the congregation is the third, all facing the communion table or altar as the focal point. The minister, or ministers, also will have seats facing toward the center of the church and located near the lectern and pulpit, so that, when not actively leading some definite part of the service they, too, are sharing in it along with the choir and congregation. And by this very symbol, incidentally, the people in the church now become a congregation rather than an audience! Audiences listen to lectures and concerts but when a group of people gather to worship they are not an audience but a congregation, literally a flock gathered together, seeking to be led by the great Shepherd of their souls.

The chancel has other, but still important, values. When combined with a proper center aisle it makes possible an effective processional. Anyone who has seen the struggles of a processional in a church without center aisle or chancel sometimes trembles for the outcome as the choir, in two single files, threads its way down two diagonal side aisles, disappears out through the doors beside the pulpit and finally reëmerges triumphantly, and still singing, through two doors in the gallery and so down to rest at last in the choir loft behind the minister! It is an adventurous pilgrimage and, I fear, more diverting than inspiring to the congregation; quite different from the dignified progressive movement up through the center of the church directly into the sanctuary which a center aisle and chancel arrangement make possible.

When it comes to weddings, funerals or the presentation of religious drama, the value of a chancel is made doubly clear. There is no pulpit in the center to be banished or camouflaged but the whole arrangement fits at once most admirably into the needs of the occasion.

But are there no limitations, dangers or difficulties about the chancel type of choir, pulpit and communion table? Indeed there are, and they need to be understood and reckoned with. Probably the greatest will be the fear of at least some in the congregation lest by this arrangement they push preaching into a secondary place and exalt the priest at the expense of the prophet. After all, your central pulpit dominating the scene is a symbol that what is expected is a prophetic ministry. The answer to this is that by exalting Christ you ought to prepare the way for prophetic preaching. Surely a cross and communion table are more prophetic symbols than organ pipes and a restless choir. And when the worship service has prepared the hearts of the people for the sermon and the preacher comes into a pulpit which is reserved for preaching and dedicated to it, then he is rightly at the focus of attention. Close to his congregation, with no moving picture background of a choir behind him, he ought now to be able to preach with all the fire and ardor for which a sincere and humble worship service has prepared the hearts of his people.

Another objection may arise from the choir director. He may say: "I need to have my choir in a semi-circle before me so that I can guide them with my baton." The answer here is: But is that advantage so great that it must be purchased at the price of distracting the congregation and destroying the atmosphere of worship? As a matter of fact, with a careful arrangement of mirrors invisible to the congregation, everyone can see the organist or director easily without his being observable by the people in the pews. Indeed, the two sides of the chancel serve to gather the choir into a united group facing each other, like a group gathered around a piano so that a unity is established; and, not having to look at an audience, the choir becomes less self-conscious and more likely to do itself justice, singing unto the Lord in the intimate fellowship of the chancel sanctuary.

Other difficulties may arise when people do not know how to use the chancel arrangement, as when the choir or a soloist think it necessary to face toward, or half-way toward, the congregation when singing instead of facing each other straight across the chancel. Sometimes a quartet will insist on coming out into the middle of the chancel so that the congregation will be sure to hear them. They need not have worried! The congregation would have enjoyed hearing them more had it seen them less and been freer to worship God. A similar difficulty of psychological adjustment is when you have the choir in its proper place but the chair for the minister is arranged so that he can still face the congregation and preside over it, the observed of all observers, whereas he ought to be merged with the congregation and the choir by occupying a seat which faces toward the center like all the other seats in the chancel.

In constructing the chancel there are certain perils to be guarded against. One is the closing off of the chancel from the church by a high rail, rood-screen or other barrier.

Churches of definitely protestant tradition will want to keep the chancel as open and free from barriers as possible. Especially will this be true in Baptist, Presbyterian, Congregational and Disciples churches where the people do not come up to an altar rail to receive communion but are served by the deacons as they sit quietly in their pews. The danger of obstructions may also arise from inexperienced architects who make the lectern and pulpit so large or place them in such a position that they block a clear view of the communion table. The lectern should be relatively small and the pulpit, while it should be large enough to be dignified and impressive, should be kept far enough to one side to allow a free and unimpeded view of the altar or communion table. There is also the problem of elevations to be studied. In general the floor of the chancel in an ordinary church should be only two or three steps above the church floor. The choir pews may be one or two steps above the chancel floor, the communion table also one or two steps above it, the lectern on a corresponding level, and even the pulpit need not be more than one or two steps higher, say from five to seven steps above the floor of the church, except in the case of a very long nave indeed.

A modification of the chancel plan which has much to commend it, especially in the case of larger churches, is the arrangement whereby the portion of the chancel occupied by the choir is screened off from the nave; partially, as in the First Congregational Church of Los Angeles; or wholly, as in the Memorial Church at Harvard University. This arrangement will appeal to choir directors because it leaves the choir to do its singing grouped in a semi-circle around the leader who is entirely free to use all the gestic-

ulation he desires without feeling that he is doing anything
distracting to the congregation. The choir, also, under these
circumstances, being largely or wholly invisible to the congregation, is more or less delivered from the concert psychology and is free from the discomfort of being always
under inspection. To the congregation the effect, if the
music is ethereally beautiful, may be like that experienced
in an Eastern Orthodox Cathedral. There the choir is invisible and even the altar is behind a beautiful door which
is opened only for the liturgy which is conducted by the
priest within the sanctuary. This solution to the problem,
by making the choir invisible, has the advantage of con-
centrating attention on the music rather than on those who
are producing it, of giving the choir-leader the best possible
control over his choir, and of keeping central before the
people the altar or communion table which stands in the
center of the chancel just forward of the screen behind
which the choir is singing.

What are the difficulties of this plan? The chief one
would seem to be psychological. Doesn't it separate the
choir too greatly from the minister and congregation and
tend to develop a detached professional attitude? Even if
the choir-master is able to maintain perfect discipline, do
not the members of the choir tend to feel, as to the rest of
the service, that they are out of it, hidden as they are behind a screen? Is not the spirit of protestant worship vio-
lated by the presence of professional singers who have no
real interest, or even possibility of participation, in the
service apart from their own professional contribution? Is
not the ideal rather that the choir, as members of the whole
group of worshippers, should lead the congregation in a

common experience of worship in all of which all of them participate? For this reason the solution at the University of Chicago chapel would seem preferable. There the singers, except a few in the chancel who lead the hymns, are located in a high gallery at the rear. They are unseen by the congregation. Their music floats down from on high like an angelic benediction. But, when not singing, they can hear the prayers and see and hear the preacher and be just as much a part of the congregation as anybody else.

In the whole matter of church architecture it is obvious that ministers, building committees and even local architects often need the advice and guidance of specialists in this field. Fortunately this is now available through the bureau of church architecture which has been set up by the Federal Council of Churches at 297 Fourth Avenue, New York, in charge of Rev. E. M. Conover. Here all who seek to build new churches or recondition old ones can obtain helpful ideas in the form of pictures and floor plans at little or no expense.

CHAPTER SEVEN

Worship Through Symbols

BEFORE WE CAN ADEQUATELY EVALUATE the materials to be used in worship we need to realize that they are all symbols and that an appreciation of symbolism is the best key to the real meaning and intelligent construction of a worship service. Broadly speaking, a symbol is something which says more than it seems to say, something which is important, or loved or cherished, or even feared and hated, because it has an aura of meaning not resident in itself alone but conferred upon it by the association of ideas which it awakens. A flag, a trademark, a wedding ring, a red and green stop-light are obvious examples of our constant use of symbols in the conduct of daily life. Clothes are symbolic of sex or wealth or taste or occupation. Each trade, profession, art or sport has its symbols, some generally recognized and others which are much more subtle and really appreciated and understood only by adepts or professionals. A boat is a symbol universally understood but what is it to "careen" a ship or "pull in your sheet" or "put over your tiller"? Only sailors know. This is because language, too, is symbolic. In fact it is hardly anything else! Except for a few emotional ejaculations, the sounds we make in speaking might mean almost anything according to our interpretations of them agreed upon in advance. Ohio, for instance, in the English language, means one of the most important of the United States but in Japanese it merely means good morning! The man who said, rather bitterly, that the purpose of language was evidently to conceal thought, probably had experienced the difficulties which words present because, as symbols, their content of meaning may be slightly, or even widely, different between two speakers. Words, therefore, are rich or poor in symbolic meaning according to their history and age-long associations with human life and also in accordance with the experience and understanding of those who use them. Barn, for instance, is a word with a much longer history, and much richer in associations and racial memories, than hangar. But a modern air-pilot's child, brought up opposite an aviation field, who had never seen a barn except looking down upon it from his father's airplane would not think so. Expressions like barn-storming, well-filled barns, barnyard ethics, wide as a barn door, a barnlike interior, big as a barn, would mean almost nothing to such a child. Symbols have meaning for two people, or a group of people, only when they grow out of a common experience and have a generally accepted interpretation.

In using the materials of worship, therefore, we must always keep in mind criteria like these: What depth and richness of hidden meaning, or what distasteful and even repellent ideas, are associated with this particular word or phrase or object or liturgical action? And, beyond this, how conscious of these deeper or associated meanings are the people whom we are trying to serve? And, finally, how can the form and content of our worship service be given greater significance for them, so that its meaningful associations may reach out into life on every side?

The protestant minister may well ask himself how far the people in his congregation really understand their own service of worship. And, if he could see into their minds and find that they were just listening to pious phrases without attaching much definite meaning to them, what should he do about it? Educate them as to the depths of meaning in words and actions too much taken for granted? Or introduce new words and actions dipped out of the current of their own life which they could not fail to understand? Or might he not well do both?

WORSHIP AS A DEED

With this understanding of the part that symbolism plays in all of life, let us ask ourselves: What are the materials to be used in worship, what values and also what dangers due to their symbolic reference, do they hold? The earliest of all worship materials are deeds and actions. Worship was something done long before it was something spoken, as Professor G. A. Johnston Ross has well pointed out in his Harvard lectures on *Christian Worship and Its Future.* Worship and magic are hard to separate in primitive religion and both were originally something done rather than something said. Even if something was said, the important thing was not merely the content of meaning but quite as much the precise way in which the saying of it was done. When words came into worship they added much, of course. They made it possible to interpret and enrich the meaning of what was done and supplement it and load new meaning into it. In this way progress became possible, for, as old meanings proved intolerable, outgrown or repellent, new and more helpful meanings could be substituted. Thus the act remained more or less unchanged, but the meaning, the value to the worshipper, changed immensely.

Now what are some of the ritual deeds which still underlie our protestant church worship? Putting on clean clothes, leaving our homes and going to a special place or building appointed for a worship service is one of them. Another form of worship by deeds is observance of the Sabbath, no matter how sketchily carried out—a day when the routine of the work-a-day week is broken and we achieve a freedom from certain kinds of slavery, a day for the lost causes of the soul, when something within us is set free. The congregation itself, the gathering together of people with some sort of common spiritual objective, just "going to church," is a very impressive deed—so impressive that it is, of course, forbidden in times of religious persecution. Then what the congregation does, its silence, its song, its common utterance, its kneeling or standing, its baring of heads, (or, in Jewish synagogues, its covering of heads), its bowing toward the altar or to receive the benediction, its filing out in silence or even its handshaking and chatter of good fellowship—all these are essentially deeds. And some of them need constant explanation or even reinterpretation to the rising generation; as, for example, the Sabbath, lest the age-long values in them be obscured and thoughtlessly cast aside. The content of meaning, the actual values and certainly the rationalizations of these actions, change from century to century, but the interesting fact is that the deeds themselves persist. They evidently have some sort of survival value deeper than any of the temporary explanations by which each age in turn has justified them.

SACRIFICE

But the greatest of all symbolic acts in worship is sacrifice. The impulse to give up something, to dedicate something to God, is at the very heart of all worship. It may be the fruits of the earth, the firstling of the flock, even the first-born child. It may be the enemy taken in warfare or the money made by trade or toil, or the work of art set up beside the altar, or the solo sung, or the life consecrated to holiness, truth and goodness—all this will vary according to the age and environment of the worshipper, but there can hardly be any true worship where the element of sacrifice is absent. In Roman Catholic worship the element of sacrifice is made central by the offering of the body, blood and divinity of Christ in the mass. What comparable symbolic act is there in protestant worship? To some extent, at least, sacrifice may be represented in the dedication of the offering. Money is a dominant symbol in our commercialized civilization and the offering presents a strategic opportunity to challenge people's calloused thoughts and easy-going ways concerning it. Money represents labor, self-denial, thrift, struggle, suffering. It may have been obtained at the cost of injustice or heartless indifference to social wrongs or even at the cost of personal integrity. Properly scrutinized, interpreted and glorified, the giving of money in an offering might be far more spiritually stimulating and more productive of deep searching of heart than any passive acceptance of a vicarious miracle wrought by a priest upon an altar. Perhaps protestantism has, in what is so often casually spoken of as "the collection," a bit of contemporary symbolism which might sting the modern conscience wide awake. But, if so, it will have to be surrounded with less pomp and more real dignity and spiritual interpretation than at present. A ritual of cleansing, of economic and financial ideals and of dedication is greatly needed for this part of the service. Charles W. Merriam did this effectively in the services he arranged for Park Church, Grand Rapids, Michigan, when he made the reception of the offering the final and climactic act in the order of morning worship. But others will need to work on this problem, too.

Greater and deeper, however, than the giving of anything material is the sacrifice of a humble and a contrite heart. Unless the worship services of a church awaken the mood and provide the opportunity for self-dedication, that church has failed adequately to recognize the absolutely fundamental quality of sacrifice in worship. Canon Donaldson has said, with penetrating insight, that one of the most menacing superficialities of our age is the all too prevalent idea that we can have worship without sacrifice.

Other symbolic acts, of which our protestant worship makes too little use, are kneeling and silence. I suspect that the average protestant worshipper really longs to kneel but does not quite know how! The pews are not equipped with kneeling stools, for one thing, and, anyhow, "it just isn't done." Indeed, a surprising and shocking proportion of some congregations sit bolt upright and even gaze about during the prayer. Perhaps if the minister knelt for a moment before the communion table or even stood silently facing it when he first entered the chancel, as is customary in Lutheran churches, it might induce a greater willingness to assume an attitude of reverence on the part of the congregation. We know that, in other areas of life, physical attitudes prepare the way for mental and emotional responses. Why should it be that only in worship we neglect this well-established principle of human nature? If we can say "hats off!" when the flag goes by, if we can rise when a lady enters the room, if we can sing and read about kneeling, why should we not actually do it as a symbolic act of reverence to God? Has our protestant reaction to Rome not carried us too far if it robs us of an inherited symbolic gesture far older than Rome? "Oh, come, let us worship and bow down, let us kneel before the Lord our maker," was written long before the pope was ever heard of. People used to kneel at family prayers in the most puritan of homes—why should they not kneel in church?

SILENCE

Silence, as an act of corporate worship, has been, of course, most appreciated and used by the Society of Friends, but it is not, and certainly should not be, their sole possession. Only those who have actually experienced the silence of a Friends' Meeting can fully realize what it may do for the peace and quiet of the soul. It has a different quality from being silent in solitude. You sit in a clean and plainly furnished room with others engaged in the same high quest. By your common silence you make, jointly with others, your spiritual gesture of recognition of a greater spiritual reality, you invite something nobler than you were before to come and dwell within you and you wait in quiet expectancy for the clearing away of spiritual dust and fog and the emergence of the dawn.

I have in my library a book, *The Ministry of Silence*, which describes what happened when a Quaker meeting house in New Zealand burned down and a neighboring Anglican church hospitably invited the Quakers to use their house of worship. The Quakers met in the vestry, as best suited to their simple type of service. But, when the vestry had to be rebuilt and redecorated, they moved up into the church itself. Then two remarkable things happened. First of all, the Friends found a certain enrichment to their quiet meditation in the presence of the age-long symbols of the Christian faith; and, equally significant, members of the Anglican communion found it satisfying to drop in at the Friends' Meeting where, amid hallowed surroundings, they could meditate with fellow believers, without the disturbing necessity of always being either talked to or saying something themselves or getting up or kneeling down.

I wonder if the truly catholic church of tomorrow will not have a chapel for silent meetings after the manner of the Friends? But silence is also a very useful element in almost any service of worship provided it is not too long continued, and provided the purpose of it and how long it is to continue are both made clear to the congregation so they are not distracted by speculations as to what is going to happen next. One of the most effective uses of silence is in connection with what is called "the bidding prayer," a form much more common in England than in this country. Here the minister indicates a series of subjects for prayerful meditation or objects for petition, pausing after each one for a period of quiet during which the worshippers may direct their personal silent prayers along the lines suggested. This is very effective if the periods of silence are not too long and if the suggestions given are concrete and vivid and of a quality which stimulates the spiritual aspiration of the worshippers. An example of a bidding prayer will be given later on when the subject of prayer is under consideration.

THE PROCESSIONAL

One more form of worship without words, where the deed counts for more than what is said, is the procession. There is something which profoundly stirs the imagination in the spectacle of an orderly group of people marching together. Militarists and nationalists know this; but the protestant church has almost forgotten it. A processional going up the church aisle into a well ordered chancel is a touch of pageantry which says in language deeper than words: "Let us go unto the house of the Lord" . . . "Send out thy light and thy truth, let them lead me. Oh, let them lead me to thy holy hill" . . . "Praise waiteth for thee, O God, in Zion; and unto thee shall the vow be performed. O thou that hearest prayer, unto thee shall all flesh come." The souls of the congregation somehow accompany a solemn orderly processional up into the place of worship. And then, when the service is over, the recessional symbolizes the return to the common tasks of life. To quote the beautiful inscriptions which Von Ogden Vogt has had carved over the entrance and exit of his church, the processional ought to say to the sensitive and the devout:

"Up from the world of the many,
To the over-world of the One."

While the recessional after worship says:

"Back to the world of the many,
To fulfill the life of the One."

SYMBOLISM AND IDOLATRY

The use of objective and visible symbols is, like the ritual deed, a primitive element in worship and yet one which we can hardly do without. Just as prayer and incantation, ritual acts and magic, are hard to differentiate in early forms of worship, so idolatry and the symbolic use of visible objects are almost inextricably intertwined.

Symbolism becomes idolatry when we honor the thing itself rather than the truth it symbolizes. There is a very illuminating story in the Old Testament about the brazen serpent. Used by Moses in the wilderness as a symbol of God's forgiveness and healing power, it became in later years merely an idol. Hezekiah, the reformer, had to destroy it. He broke it in pieces and called it: "Nehushtan— a piece of brass"! [1] When symbols become idols, then some iconoclast comes along and reveals that they are only pieces of brass after all! The trouble with idols is that they stop thought and arrest progress, whereas a true symbol stimulates thought and makes progress easier. In the whole matter of worship we have to be constantly on guard against the peril of degenerating into idolatry, the idolatry of buildings, of creeds, of liturgies, of prayer books, of vestments, and even of ecclesiastical functionaries. Human nature always tends to slip into externalism, an insistence on outward forms and ceremonies which ends in the blind alley

[1] II Kings 18:4.

of sacerdotalism. But, on the other hand, these accessories of worship are necessary and, indeed, inevitable. The only hope is to keep them as living symbols rather than dead idols.

THE CROSS

Nowhere is this more true than in the physical objects employed in worship. Let us consider some of them. The most conspicuous object used as a symbol in Christian worship is the cross. It needs constant reinterpretation. One person may see in it a symbol of some outgrown theory of the atonement quite repellent to most of us. But it may also be a symbol of the sacredness of vicarious suffering as exemplified by Jesus, a recognition of the tragic element in life and of the necessity of sacrifice in all human service and salvation. It may be supremely the symbol of the spirit and character of Jesus, and a reminder of the hardships which justice, love and goodness undergo in a wicked world. Its depths of meaning will be proportionate to the depth of our understanding of Christ himself.

The attitude of many protestants toward the cross is curiously inconsistent, due to anti-Roman Catholic prejudices inherited from the reformation. The Catholics have indeed, almost succeeded in taking possession of the cross as a denominational emblem! But this only in certain external forms and visible uses. Many a protestant congregation will sing lustily, "In the cross of Christ, I glory" or "At the cross, at the cross, where I first saw the light," and yet react violently against a proposal to place a cross on the communion table. Other congregations, which easily enough tolerate or even approve a cross on the communion table,

would yet hesitate to have one carried at the head of a processional at morning worship. A story is told of a choir
which at the last minute was refused permission to carry
in the processional a cross which they had already pro-
cured and expected to use. Obliged by action of the church
officers to leave it in the choir-room, they marched in singing vociferously:

> "Onward, Christian soldiers, marching as to war,
>   With the cross of Jesus, hid behind the door!"

If the cross is to be used as a visible symbol, however,
and not just sung about or preached about, certain pre-
cautions are necessary. Do not have too many crosses and
do not have them too large, or too small either. I know of
a Catholic church where the cross on the spire is so large
that it dwarfs the spire and of a protestant church where
the cross on the altar is so small that it looks like a toy!
The design of the cross is important, also. It ought not to
be too square and heavy but tall and slender. A cross of
the Iona or Celtic type seems to have more protestant associations than the plain Latin cross, though both may be
used. Over-ornateness should be avoided. For a communion
table a very simple inexpensive cross can easily be provided by having it made carefully to scale by a good cab-
inet maker, then staining or painting it to match the woodwork of the church, and then just faintly outlining it in
gold with a quarter inch edging of gold paint. The other
side can be done all in gold, if desired, and reserved for
use at Christmas and Easter and weddings. In any case,
an empty cross rather than a crucifix with the agonized
body of Jesus still hanging on it is preferable, for protes-

tants at least. To us the cross should be not only the symbol of Jesus' death, but of his continued presence and influence. An empty cross is a triumphal cross. The light of the Easter morning is shining on it. The scaffold of the Roman Empire has become a thing of beauty, the symbol of one whose message and meaning it could not kill.

PULPIT AND LECTERN

Other physical symbols of value in protestant worship are the communion table and chalice and the baptismal font, of which we shall speak in the chapter on the sacraments. Still others, which must be considered briefly here, however, are the pulpit and the lectern.

The pulpit symbolizes the prophetic utterance of truth as the Holy Spirit gives the preacher utterance. It should, therefore, be large enough to dignify its function, and so placed and illuminated that the preacher can easily be heard and seen. It ought to be equipped with a shelf, hidden from view but containing a glass of water for emergency use, and an electric or other clock should be so built into the top of it as to be plainly visible to the preacher, but to no one else! If any wall clock is used in the church, it should be on the back wall, never in easy view of the congregation.

The lectern should be distinctly smaller than the pulpit, but the Bible on it should not be small. It should, by its very size, suggest something of the grandeur of the scriptures and the veneration which attaches to them. Above all, the lectern should not be empty! I know of a college chapel which has an elaborate lectern in the form of a great brass eagle with outstretched wings and a menacing beak. I do not altogether admire this lectern, personally preferring simpler designs, but it would be much less conspicuous if it held a great Bible, large enough, when opened, to extend from tip to tip of the wings. If this were done, the function of the eagle would be clear and the Bible would receive the mind's attention.

CHOIR GOWNS

Finally, remembering that clothes are symbols, we come to the question of how choir and minister should dress when conducting worship services. The advantage of a uniform costume for the choir is pretty generally recognized. It promotes democracy and esprit de corps. It delivers the congregation from eccentricity or poor taste in dress or colors on the part of choir members and it adds to the dignity of the occasion, especially if there be a processional. But, if the choir is to be gowned, there should be a mistress of the robes or a committee to keep the vestments·clean, mended and in good order. The simplest and easiest choir robes to install and maintain are of the same design as college gowns, although they may not necessarily be in black. Purple, maroon and blue are also used. Such gowns may be ordered from dealers or even made by the women of the church very inexpensively of unbleached material and then dyed the desired color. In any case the women should wear large flat white sailor collars and the men should uniformly wear white shirts and collars and dark ties, if ties are visible. Gowns worn over a variety of colored collars, or by women with no collars at all, present a very unkempt appearance, whereas a vested choir should always appear neat and uniform. The women also may wear caps, the Canterbury cap with its softer lines being preferable to the collegiate mortar-board. A very popular alternative to the college gown type of vestment is the white surplice worn over a cassock of black or purple or maroon as may be desired, the women's caps matching the cassock. This has the advantage of brightness, the white surplices standing out against the soft light and shadows of the church; but such a uniform should not be adopted unless the surplices are sure to be kept scrupulously fresh and clean.

THE MINISTER'S GOWN

What shall the minister wear? If the choir is not vested, he may wear a plain dark suit of black or dark blue or oxford gray, with a plain dark tie, black shoes and socks and no watch chain or conspicuous jewelry. Simplicity, modesty and inconspicuousness spell good taste for the minister on all occasions, but especially when conducting public worship. If the choir is robed, however, he certainly ought also to wear a gown, bachelor's, master's or doctor's, appropriate to his academic degree. An ordinary choir gown will do, but it should be black and generally of a little finer material, mohair or poplin will do quite as well as silk. The black, so-called Geneva gown for protestant ministers goes back to the reformation and the protest in both Calvinistic and Lutheran circles against medieval sacerdotalism with its elaborate and gorgeous vestments which set the priest apart from the common people. The reformers, emphasizing the priesthood of all believers, had their ministers dress, not in the ancient priestly vestments, but in the proper garb of an educated man, which was the academic gown. Such a gown was worn by both Luther and Calvin and by William Bradford when he conducted the services of our Pilgrim Fathers after they landed from the *Mayflower*. The idea, which seems to be popularly held in some places, that wearing a gown indicates a drift toward Rome is, therefore, quite unfounded in history. It is just the other way. The black scholar's gown is the traditional dress of the protestant minister and indicates that we expect our ministers to be scholarly and educated men. Occasionally some protestant ministers wear a stole, a narrow band of silk, black or white or colored and usually with a cross or other symbol embroidered on it. The stole hangs over the neck and down in front on either side. This is a true ecclesiastical vestment and indicates that the wearer is a minister engaged in conducting a worship service. It adds a desirable touch of color to the rather somber black gown. In Central Union Church, Honolulu, the ministers wear a cream-colored, light-weight, silk gown with a black stole about four inches wide, which makes an excellent combination, especially in a tropical climate, and one that might well be used anywhere. Whatever color of gown is worn, it can be fitted with sleeves and buttoned down the front like a cassock so that, in warm weather, the wearer can remove both coat and vest before putting on the gown and thus wear no heavier clothing than necessary. If called upon to wear any head covering at all, the minister should use a college cap, never a biretta. Percy Dearmer, who is an authority on such things, says that even in an Anglican church a biretta is utterly out of place, being a distinctly Roman bit of ecclesiastical headgear.

Perhaps this section on clerical sartorial proprieties may

best draw to a close with a word of protest against the half-way custom, prevalent in so many churches, of robing the choir and even having them march in in a processional, and then leaving the minister in morning coat or sack suit to wander in by himself before or after the choir has entered. The minister who has a vested choir should have the courage to wear a gown himself. And if the choir marches in, he should come in following it as the last person in the processional.

Should the minister wear his academic hood? In Britain it is customary; and the habit is increasing in the eastern part of the United States, especially in college chapels. A conservative practice would be to reserve the hood for an added touch of color at Christmas, Easter, weddings and academic occasions like a baccalaureate sermon. Hoods are not restricted to doctors or masters but anyone with a B.D. degree is entitled to wear the hood of that degree, which, with its cardinal red velvet collar, gives a desirable touch of color to a black gown. If anyone objects that the minister's wearing anything other than ordinary street clothes in the pulpit is just play-acting and therefore artificial and insincere, I would suggest that he ponder what G. A. Johnston Ross once said to me on this subject: "Clothes ought to be appropriate to what one is doing. I wear a bathing suit to go in swimming, denim overalls to work on my car, sports clothes to play golf and a tuxedo when invited out to dinner. Why should I not also wear appropriate and traditional garments when engaged in leading a congregation in the worship of God—especially when such garments reduce my personal eccentricities of dress or form and exalt or dignify the act I am performing?"

EMMANUEL
SCHOOL OF RELIGION
~ LIBRARY

CHAPTER EIGHT

The Words of Worship

EPISCOPALIANS AND LUTHERANS have the advantage of a fixed liturgy. It is an advantage in that it secures uniformity. The worshipper knows that the service will have essentially the same content whether in a cathedral or on a ship crossing the Atlantic. It also has the advantage of a high level of literary excellence. The Episcopal prayer book is one of the great classics of the English tongue and is akin to Shakespeare and the King James version of the Bible in its formative effect upon our literature. No service can go far wrong or sink into utter depths of vulgarity or inanity if it follows the prayer book or the Lutheran ritual.

But, although this be granted cheerfully enough, it still remains true that such a prescribed ritual may be also in some respects a handicap. Its literary grandeur may all too evidently date it as belonging to an age long past so that the service loses that vivid and vital note of contemporaneousness which the worshipper craves in his approach to God. And, while good taste will always be preserved, something of the tang of present day reality and these bitter times which try men's souls will be lost. Worship must have as deep and rich a background of the past as it is possible to give it. There is a place in it for ancient symbolism, ancient creeds and formulas, ancient language and terminology, and especially for ancient music. The very word venerable is woven into our conception of worship. If we do not venerate the past we lose an untold treasure. But, at the same time, to be at its best and achieve its real purpose, the worship service must be something more than a reading of the minutes of the last meeting, no matter how important or beautiful that meeting may have been! It must move on to new business and hold a significant and stirring meeting of its own. Important things have happened in the world of religious thought since the prayer book was crystallized into its present form. Men need to meditate and pray in terms of the hopes and fears which are round about them, some of which Cranmer and Martin Luther, happily, never had to face.

Upon the non-liturgical or free churches there rests, therefore, a great responsibility which is at the same time a magnificent opportunity. It is their privilege to create liturgical forms in which ancient and modern materials can both be used, and to give the worship service a growing edge by incorporating into it what is best and most challenging and inspiring in modern religious thought and literature. The alert minister, like the scribe of old who brought out of his treasure things new and old, and thereby won Jesus' commendation, will always be on the lookout for a poem, a prayer, or a prose passage which sounds an authentic note of modern need and contemporary aspiration that he may build it into his worship service for the comfort and edification of his congregation. They will recognize it and say: "There, that is just what we face today! There is help out of Zion for our modern difficulties after all!" As an illustration of this I would quote my experience in attending church some time ago, after a week in which the world had been following with agonized attention the newspaper reports of a hunger-strike down in the pit by some desperate ill-paid miners in central Europe. It was a stroke of genius when the minister brought to us, as his extra-Biblical reading for that morning, Louis Untermeyer's poignant poem, "Caliban in the Coal Mines," which ends, as you will remember, with that great line,

"Lord, fling us a handful of stars"!

BIBLICAL MATERIAL

Remembering, therefore, the scribe who, as Jesus noticed, brought out of his treasures things new and old, we who lead public worship today should consider what words of worship, both ancient and modern, are ours to employ. We begin, therefore, with the Bible. Here is a veritable mine of material, only a part of which has been adequately appreciated and drawn upon thus far in the history of Christian worship. The Psalms, to be sure, have been largely used, but sometimes without proper discrimination in view of the revengeful and unChristian character of some of them. But with that liberty of Christian choice and editing which we now have, it will not be hard to omit sub-Christian passages. What remains represents spiritual aspiration and devotion at its highest level. But, beyond the Psalms, there are notable passages in the Bible which are marvelously adapted to liturgical use but which have been neglected hitherto. In the appendix we have included a list of these passages which have particular value for unison or responsive reading. The fact that Hebrew poetry was not a matter of rhyme or meter but of parallelism and noble similes makes it more capable of translation than the poetry of any other language; and it also means that many passages which have been printed as prose, notably in the prophets, really are religious poetry of the highest order.

CHRISTIAN DEVOTIONAL LITERATURE

In addition to the Bible, we are free to draw upon the great liturgies of Christendom, which contain prayers, responses, litanies, and benedictions hallowed by age and the use of countless thousands of believers. The creeds and confessions of Christendom are also ours to use with the same privilege of review and editorial judgment that we have already exercised regarding the Old Testament. Beyond these formal documents of the church lies a great mass of devotional literature which is also ours to appraise and employ. This includes the great hymns, and classics of the devotional life such as St. Augustine's "Confessions," St. Francis' "Canticle of the Sun," St. Thomas à Kempis' "Imitation of Christ," Bunyan's "Pilgrim's Progress," and poems of all the Christian centuries from Piers Ploughman and Chaucer (in translation) to Oxenham and Masefield, including Milton, Browning and Tennyson along the way.

Nor is modern prose to be neglected. Some of it, notably by Tolstoy, Lincoln, Lowell and others, has a dignity and rhythm similar to the Bible. Thirkield and Huckel in their *Book of Common Worship* have given an excellent example, in their eighth and ninth orders of worship, of what noble use can be made of ancient material, some of it quite unknown to the modern church, rescued from the early centuries of the Christian era. The use which can be made of modern writings is equally well revealed by the little book of responsive readings called, *Readings from Great Authors* and edited by John Haynes Holmes.

NON-CHRISTIAN RELIGIOUS CLASSICS

One form of literature, the use of which in Christian services of worship may raise more question, is made up of the great religious classics of other faiths. Robert E. Hume in his *Treasure House of the World Religions* has given us a choice selection of the best which the non-Christian religions have to offer, and men of worldwide sympathies and universal temper will find here fresh and helpful approaches to certain great truths which are common to us all. That other religions share these ideas is something to be regarded with joy and on no account to be concealed. In these days when the real foe of all spiritual religion is materialism, secularism, militarism and the worship of the totalitarian state, surely all the religious forces of the world should recognize and occupy all the common ground they can. To employ in the worship of God and for the inspiration of humanity the high and uplifting utterances of other denominations and even of other religions would seem to be the true spirit of the largest ecumenicity. Therefore, if Confucius, or Buddha, or Lao Tse or Mohammed or Maimonides or the Talmud have given beautiful expression to some universal truth why should we pass it by? The question is not: Who wrote it? so much as: Is it true? Is it Christian? Is it said with such beauty and distinction that it will deepen and adorn our service of Christian worship? Of course, nothing ought to be used, whatever its origin, if it does not pass these tests.

UNISON AND RESPONSIVE READINGS

If then all things are ours, so long as we are Christ's and Christ is God's, how shall we use this wealth of the world's great literature of devotion? First of all for readings, individual, unison or responsive. We come to church, in part, to be reminded of the great truths of our holy religion. Even if the sermon is a failure, these great classic utterances may do for us what we needed, after all. And what is equally important, some things which might irritate and produce swift and unfavorable reactions if the minister said them on his own authority, may command a more receptive hearing when read in the words of someone long since dead but of recognized and assured wisdom who could not have had us personally in mind but who dealt our pride or prejudice a mighty blow, nevertheless.

Such readings, however, should not be too long, especially if they are to be read in unison. There is something very impressive about unison readings, if the material selected is not too involved and has a rhythm and cadence easy for the group to feel and follow. The same is true of responsive readings. The portions for both the leader and the congregation should neither of them be too long, nor too short either, but it is especially important that the congregation's responses should be short and rhythmic. Much responsive reading is really just alternative reading. The leader reads a sentence and then the people read a sentence and so on. But responsive readings are most effective and artistic when they partake more of the character of a litany so that what the people say is a real response or reaction to what the leader has said. To illustrate this more clearly, contrast a reading of the beatitudes in which the leader and congregation simply each read a beatitude, turn and turn about, with the following setting where what the people respond helps to emphasize and bring deeper home the beatitude which the leader has just read.

THE BEATITUDES WITH RESPONSES

Blessed are the poor in spirit: for theirs is the kingdom of heaven.

Lord, have mercy upon us, and gather us with all who seek the humble and contrite heart.

Blessed are they that mourn: for they shall be comforted.

Bring those of us who mourn, O Lord, into the healing shadow of thy love.

Blessed are the meek: for they shall inherit the earth.

Lord, have mercy upon us, and deliver us from all contention and false pride.

Blessed are they that hunger and thirst after righteousness: for they shall be filled.

Feed our hungry souls, O Lord, upon the bread of life.

Blessed are the merciful: for they shall obtain mercy.

Lord, have mercy upon us, and incline our hearts toward all tenderness and love.

Blessed are the pure in heart: for they shall see God.

Dwell thou within our hearts, and let us see thee everywhere.

Blessed are the peacemakers: for they shall be called sons of God.

Give unto us an understanding heart and patient spirit that we may follow after peace and pursue it.

Blessed are they that have been persecuted for righteousness sake: for theirs is the kingdom of God.

Have mercy upon us, O Lord, and make us more worthy of the martyrs who have gone before us.

Blessed are ye when men shall reproach you and persecute you, and say all manner of evil against you falsely, for my sake. Rejoice and be exceedingly glad: for great is your reward in heaven.

Lord keep us faithful even unto death and bring us at last to thine eternal city.

VERSICLES AND RESPONSES

The subject of unison and responsive readings suggests the very ancient usage of reciting a creed or confession of faith and of giving the congregation a chance to respond by the use of versicles like "Glory be to Thee" or responses as when the leader says, "The Lord be with you," and the congregation replies, "And with thy spirit," or the leader says, "Praise ye the Lord," and the congregation replies, "The Lord's name be praised." Such responses may be either said or sung but they do provide needed introductions or transitions and keep alive the sense of participation on the part of the congregation. They are very ancient and for that reason, also, are appealing to all who have or can attain to the historical mind. Now that the gloria is so widely used, let us hope that the value and beauty of these versicles and responses may obtain for them also a more general acceptance. A service of worship should flow, and to flow each element in it must be appropriately introduced without abrupt changes or jarring announcements. Herein lies the great liturgical value of these versicles. They may be used to provide introductions or transitions to new moods in the service in a beautiful and natural way that strikes no discordant note.

CONFESSIONS OF FAITH

There is great emotional and unifying value in having a congregation rise up and make confession of their common faith in noble and historic language, and then all join in singing the gloria. Such an act binds people together in common loyalty to their faith and to the past. It gives them a sense of community with the prophets, apostles, saints and martyrs of the long ago, and with all their fellow seekers after spiritual truth today. It is, therefore, a most valuable part of Christian worship in an age and country where we have altogether too little sense of social solidarity and historical background. But, valuable as such a recitation of the creed or some other confession of faith may be, it is dying out.

The reason is not difficult to find. It lies primarily in the incongruity or assumed conflict between the Apostles' Creed and modern ways of thinking about religious truth and spiritual values. Some would go further and say it is due to the unwillingness of the skeptical modern temper to come down to rest on any positive affirmations about anything. "Nobody believes anything any more," such critics would say, "the props have been knocked out from under all inherited assumptions. It will be better to proceed tentatively without committing ourselves to anything except as a provisional hypothesis!" That this represents the attitude of some ultra-sophisticated people is doubtless true. But it is only an extreme position, a sort of pragmatism gone to seed and agnosticism elevated into a dogma! The great mass of people still believe that there are some things which are true, some principles to be adhered to; they believe that the universe really has an ethical backbone and is not just a moral and spiritual jellyfish—good for nothing and likely to sting you if you touch it!

Most people today, at least the ones likely to do anything

constructive and useful in the world, have deep basic convictions and a courageous and militant faith, and they
would feel better if they had some way of expressing that
faith in church. The trouble with the Apostles' Creed is not
so much that it is untrue—for it is, of course, capable of
such historical reinterpretation as would make it possible
for almost any intelligent and informed modern Christian
to accept it—as that it is off-center. It deals with things
which are at one side rather than in the center of our Christian faith today and even leaves out things which we count
of the greatest importance. We are concerned, for example,
not only that God is the maker of heaven and earth but that
he is the continually present and active sustaining power
within his universe. A miraculous virgin birth as the origin
of Jesus' earthly body has little interest for us, and does
not in itself give any basis for his authority in the realm
of morals and religion, while for many, trained in the rules
of scientific and historical evidence, it raises almost in-
superable difficulties. To put this belief in the creed only
creates intellectual and emotional problems and brings no
constructive values, no positive inspiration. If you say that
historically the emphasis on the virgin birth arose to
counteract docetism and make clear the union of human
and divine elements in Jesus from the very beginning, the
answer is that, however interesting such a statement may
be historically, the modern mind does not move in such a
thought world. If the human and divine are united in Jesus,
we shall be convinced of it by his character, his words,
his deeds, and not by any doctrine as to the origin of his
physical body. Meanwhile the Creed suffers from a lack of
the very things which would appeal to men and women

educated along modern historical and scientific lines. It contains no reference to Jesus' teachings, character or deeds. It tells what was done to him but nothing of what he did or said in all the days of his ministry. The descent into hell and the reference to the Catholic church and the bodily resurrection also make trouble and require much explaining. And so, although the Apostles' Creed has great liturgical value and is in itself a sonorous and beautifully rhythmic utterance, the plain fact is that it is being used less and less in American churches. Its recitation alienates too many people or raises too many problems to be overcome.

What then? We still need to make confession of our faith! Only it must be *our* faith! Here is a great opportunity for some religious thinker, some truly ecumenical mind, to crystallize the best faith and noblest religious thinking of our day into a formula of supreme literary beauty which now, and perhaps for hundreds of years to come, might serve as a brief and well-rounded liturgical expression of the things which are most certainly believed among us.

As a hopeful illustration of what has already been done in this direction the Statement of Faith adopted by the National Council of Congregational Churches, meeting at Kansas City in 1916, may be cited:

A STATEMENT OF FAITH

We believe in God the Father, infinite in wisdom, goodness, and love; and in Jesus Christ, his Son, our Lord and Saviour, who for us and our salvation lived and died and rose again and liveth evermore; and in the Holy Spirit, who taketh of the things of Christ and revealeth them to us, renewing, comforting, and inspiring the souls of men.

We are united in striving to know the will of God as taught in the Holy Scriptures, and in our purpose to walk in the ways of the Lord, made known or to be made known to us.

We hold it to be the mission of the Church of Christ to proclaim the gospel to all mankind, exalting the worship of the one true God, and labouring for the progress of knowledge, the promotion of justice, the reign of peace, and the realization of human brotherhood.

Depending, as did our fathers, upon the continued guidance of the Holy Spirit to lead us into all truth, we work and pray for the transformation of the world into the kingdom of God; and we look with faith for the triumph of righteousness and the life everlasting.

*   *   *

If this be regarded as too long for liturgical uses, the following shorter form is to be commended:

We believe in God, the Father Almighty, and in Jesus Christ, his Son, our Lord, and in the Holy Spirit. We seek to know the will of God, to walk in his ways, made known or to be made known to us and to proclaim the gospel to all mankind. We work and pray for the progress of knowledge, the promotion of justice, the reign of peace, and the realization of human brotherhood. And we look with faith for the triumph of righteousness and the life everlasting.

*   *   *

Another even shorter confession of faith which has been found to be effective especially in brief services or those designed for children or young people is as follows:

We believe in the fatherhood of God and in the brotherhood of man. We believe that Christ is the way and the truth and the life. We believe in the clean heart, the unworldly life, and the service of love that Jesus taught and exemplified. We accept his spirit and his teaching and dedicate ourselves to his unfinished work.

*   *   *

Confessions of faith in scriptural language are gratefully received and occasionally a modern prose utterance like Lowell's: "God is in all that liberates and lifts," or Tolstoy's beautiful confession of faith; or a short poem like Sam Walter Foss', "And what is faith?" or Louis Untermeyer's "Ever insurgent let me be!" or John Oxenham's, "In Christ there is no east nor west," can be used as an effective liturgical expression of common faith and aspiration. Perhaps the most universally available confession of faith which people still can be depended upon to recite from memory and which, therefore, can be used in a more or less improvised service, such as a minister may be called upon to conduct at a summer camp or on a ship at sea, is the Twenty-third Psalm. One could wish that he could be equally sure of complete familiarity with the Beatitudes and the Thirteenth Chapter of First Corinthians which also would serve admirably as confessions of our faith.

ANNOUNCEMENTS

The most important of all the words used in worship are, of course, the words of prayer. So important is prayer in the worship service that the entire next chapter will be devoted to it. But there are other words which deserve attention because of the importance of their being left out! These are the words of announcement which break in upon the service and interrupt its flow. I do not speak now of a

brief period when the minister acts as a sort of animated
bulletin board and gives out the notices or, as the Scotch
so deprecatingly call them, the "intimations" of events
about to happen in the round of church activities. Something can be said for this, in spite of the way it has been
abused. Rightly located, perhaps as a sort of interlude
before the sermon, such announcements may add a very
human and heartwarming touch as the pastor makes his
comments and exhorts his people about sundry practical
matters of mutual concern. Better, of course, that all announcements should be printed or mimeographed. It is
more efficient from every viewpoint to take care of notices
this way. But, on the other hand, the service ought not to be
so stiff and formal that there is not a place where the pastor
can talk normally and naturally about things of practical
interest to the church. Even Shakespeare's tragedies have
their sub-plots and flashes of comic relief!

But what I had in mind when I suggested that words of
announcement should be minimized and, so far as possible,
omitted, was the announcement of separate items in the
service as, for example: "Let us now sing hymn 268, using
the second tune, the old familiar tune of Mendebras, but
omitting the 6th and 17th stanzas"! Or, "The Scripture
lesson will now be read by Reverend Ebenezer Smith who
has recently come to be the pastor of the Tenth Avenue
Church." Or, "We shall now be favored by a vocal selection by Miss Mary Jones." Each time such an announcement is made something happens to the spirit of the service
akin to what happens to an electric current every time the
line is grounded. Relatively plain factual announcements,
such as have just been quoted, are bad enough; but still

worse things in the announcement line may happen, as when Mary Jones is credited with being a graduate of the local Mozart Musical Conservatory, or the minister decides to pep things up a little by saying: "Now, folks, let's see if we can't put a little more life into this grand old hymn. You weren't half singing last time. Step on the gas now and open 'er up wide and let's sing till we make the rafters rattle!" Experience will demonstrate that something is lost in the total effect of a worship service every time it is brought down to earth by some prosaic announcement, whereas there is a sustained high level and cumulative spiritual impressiveness if it is avoided. Announcements have the effect of breaking up the service into a series of sharply separated events, whereas a service proceeding without announcement achieves unity, flow and climax.

How can announcements be avoided? By having the order of service so carefully mimeographed or printed that nothing more needs to be said; or by having an order of service which the people know and then placing on a hymn-board the necessary numbers of hymns and readings. Before long the congregation learns to reach for hymn books as soon as the organist begins playing the tune. Or, in very informal services where there are no hymn books, as at a retreat in some summer camp or out-of-doors, all that is necessary is for a little group of six or eight good singers to lead out bravely on hymns agreed upon in advance and all the rest will join in. Supply the little group with three or four hymn books, so they are sure of the words, and the spontaneity of the singing will make far more appeal than many wisecracks by an over-urgent song-leader. Mimeographing is not difficult and simple hymn-boards of a churchly design can be made by anyone who can handle a saw and plane. Numbers can be purchased from any church supply house and the board can be stained to match the woodwork. Anyone who has felt the improvement achieved by a service that proceeds smoothly without announcement will never want to go back to the old way of doing things.

CHAPTER NINE

Prayer as the Heart of Worship

PRAYER IS NOT ALL there is to worship; praise also has its place, and self-examination and confession and commitment; but prayer is central. Without prayer worship would be inadequate and incomplete. If the prayer, however, has been deep and sincere and in the spirit of Jesus, true worship has been achieved, no matter what shortcomings it may have in any other respects. Let us, therefore, look carefully at the prayers which are at the very heart of Christian worship, remembering that they include not only the prayers spoken by the minister and those in which the congregation joins audibly but also the silent prayers which are the worshipper's very own. Indeed is not this silent prayer by the worshippers the ultimate test as to the quality and value of the worship service? An electric current in one wire may set up and induce a current in a parallel wire. Similarly the service should inspire those in attendance to make their own prayers. If it does that it has succeeded. Otherwise it has accomplished very little.

How can this mood and atmosphere of prayer be secured? First of all, as has been indicated in earlier chapters, by the quiet, reverence, beauty and dignity, of the place where the worshipping congregation meets, and by the symbols before them and the conduct and example of minister and choir. Music will certainly help and there will need to be preparatory instruction as to the meaning and technique of worship. But, supremely, it will be the public prayers uttered by the minister or shared by the congregation that will induce the mood of personal and silent prayer. These public prayers are, therefore, vitally important.

THE LEADER'S PREPARATION FOR PUBLIC PRAYER

The person who is to conduct public worship will need to come, of course, into a clear understanding in his own mind as to what prayer is and what it may accomplish, in order that he may do the kind of praying that is proper and of value in a worship service. As already indicated in the chapter on Worship and Theology, prayer is not just intercession or petition, though these may have their place, and certainly it is not a way of compelling God to accept our judgment and do our will. Rather, shall we not say that prayer is essentially communion? Recognition of God, desire to know his will, acceptance of his way and commitment to it, repentance and the seeking of forgiveness, an open-minded quest for guidance and a deep desire for greater sensitivity to the divine presence: are not these the elements of Christian prayer which must precede, or certainly surround, petition?

The leader of public worship will probably be able to communicate to others in the worship service a sense of the reality and presence of God about in proportion as he is himself a person of devout and mystical attitudes. "In order to pray well it is necessary already to have prayed," is a wise paradoxical statement by a great European authority on worship: "Pour bien prier, il faut déjà avoir prié." [1] What is meant, I take it, is not formal verbal prayer but what von Hugel, in his marvelous little book on *The Life of Prayer* calls "the prayer of quiet." He says: "Now there is no doubt that the prayer of quiet—that a certain formless recollection and loving feeding upon the sense and presence of God—of God as here and now—is a most legitimate prayer." [2] And again: "The decisive preparation for prayer lies not in itself, but in the life prior to the prayer." [3] This is what Brother Lawrence also discovered in *The Practice of the Presence of God*.

In other words, it is necessary that the leader of worship be himself a godly man in order to be able through public prayers to make the worship service most completely an experience of God for others. You may say: What difference does the leader's own personal godliness make if he uses the right words and observes reverent attitudes, especially if the service he is following is a prescribed and printed ritual? The answer, of course, is that while, with a set liturgy, less depends on the depth of the leader's religious experience and emotional conviction, yet, even so, a lack of these things will eventually show through even the noblest ritual. It is like the difference between the same tune played on two violins, one cheaply and carelessly made and the other a masterpiece, mellow and beautiful in tone. Sooner or later the essential tone of a man's soul will steal through the music of his public prayers and people will sense the realities of spiritual experience and con-

[1] Robert Will, *Le Culte*, p. 209.
[2] Baron Friedrich von Hugel: *The Life of Prayer*, p. 44.
[3] *Ibid.*, p. 30.

viction which lie behind. Especially true and inescapable will this be if his prayers are of his own devising as they are in most non-liturgical churches.

If anyone really desires, therefore, to make his conduct of public worship a blessing to others, he must first of all cultivate and keep alive an inner mystical sense of God's presence in his own life and in the world round about him. Von Hugel's suggestion, taken from Jean Nicholas Grou, as to "the importance of the soul's possession of two levels and kinds of action and interest—a wholesome natural interest and action, and a deep supernatural interest and action," [4] is a wise insight into spiritual hygiene. Sanity and balance are thus preserved without spiritual blindness and aridity. A blend of clear-eyed discrimination and moral integrity combined with a habit of spiritual sensitivity and insight will characterize the practical mystic who is neither a cold intellectualist nor a pious fanatic. When a man of this finely balanced quality leads public worship, people find their hearts strangely warmed and the world of spiritual values becomes real and authoritative in their lives. Was not that precisely the experience people had with Phillips Brooks and still have with Schweitzer, Kagawa and E. Stanley Jones? Hence, far removed as it may seem from the practical and external things involved in conducting public worship, the maintenance of a man's own personal integrity and a life of constant communion with God are absolutely basic. The minister cannot lead a double life, cannot serve two standards of morality, cannot even view with equanimity any compromising shadow upon

[4] Baron Friedrich von Hugel, *The Life of Prayer*, p. 34.

his own transparent sincerity and honor which might prove
to be

> "That rift within the lute
> Which, slowly widening, makes the music mute."

INSIGHT INTO PEOPLE'S NEEDS

Moral integrity, however, even though combined with
genuine humility and a mystical appreciation of spiritual
values, is not all that is necessary for effective leadership
in public prayer. Insight into people's personal struggles
and a mastery of the literary technique of truly beautiful
prayers are also needed. The understanding of people's
problems comes partly from the knowledge of modern psychiatric insights into the inner conflicts and hungers of the
human personality and partly from a knowledge of the
world's great literature, especially drama and fiction,
where these inner tensions have been portrayed. But all
partial and secondhand apprehensions of the human spiritual struggle are quite in vain unless they are grounded
in a deep pastoral experience of facing life's problems
with one's parishioners and in one's own experience as
well. When a good pastor makes a really good prayer at a
Sunday morning service it does something for the worshippers which is akin to the blending of three notes to make
a rich harmonious chord. The minister whose prayers uplift his people will be one who knows his people and their
inner fears and problems and who also knows how to express the aspirations of their souls in winged words that
lift them out of the murk and fog of sordid and defeated
living into the clear sunshine of spiritual reality. Hence

public prayer is a combination of three absolutely necessary things: personal sincerity, psychological insight into
other people's needs and literary skill.

Insight into the needs of the congregation involves a
knowledge of the actual conditions which people are facing
in their daily lives and an understanding of how the human
mind reacts in the presence of difficulty and discouragement. But life is not all difficulty and discouragement, by
any means, and so the minister should also remember
youth with its boundless hopes, and the courageous fighter
in life's middle battle whose head is "bloody but unbowed." Then let him sound for them a clear bugle note
of on-going courage and constructive achievement! The
minister needs to experience life, not at secondhand but
from active participation in it, in order that he may know
when and where to sound this bugle call of courage. Literature is all very well, and often gives a profound insight
into people's hearts but, after all, as Robert Louis Stevenson once remarked, "literature is a mighty bloodless substitute for life." So the minister who plunges into life, who
is married, has children, knows poverty, goes faithfully
in and out among his parishioners and looks out through
their eyes on the personal and social problems which beset
them, is far more apt to lead them gloriously in prayer
than if he sat in some ivory tower of untroubled security
far above the battle of daily living.

TRADITIONAL LITERARY USAGE IN PRAYER

But prayer also has its literary side. Personal integrity,
mystical insight and practical experience all come to their
highest when they find adequate expression. It is not more

"mute inglorious Miltons" that we need but more articulate and contemporary Miltons who can express what the soul longs to say. Prayer is almost as definite a literary form as drama or lyric poetry or free verse or the peculiar prose of a legal document. It has its traditional usages, its underlying principles and its perils and pitfalls even as have all other literary forms. He who would lead in public worship must not despise these things.

Traditional usage requires that public prayer be cast in the quaint and antique language of Shakespeare, the Bible and the Book of Common Prayer. This has great value in added dignity and a certain distinction which is apt to be lost when translated into everyday usage. But it also means that he who leads in public prayer should take pains to master the simple grammatical inflections involved. Prayer, as addressed directly to God, should always refer to him in the second person, not in the third. When God is talked about, rather than appealed to directly and personally, it is obvious that the prayer is really being addressed to the congregation whereas it should only have gathered up the needs and hopes and fears of the congregation in order to present them before God. Prayer, of course, may be addressed to Christ, as representative of God; or to the Holy Spirit, as God's living presence in the world; but, on the whole, the Christian world does well to remember the words of Jesus: "When ye pray, say, Father." Jesus himself has warned us that prayer should be brief, avoiding vain repetitions, and that it is to be prepared for by sincere and honest living, and especially by forgiving those who have offended us.

SOME RULES OF LITERARY COMPOSITION

A few simple literary rules to be observed in formulating public prayer are these:

1. *Accent the verbs:* Verbs and nouns are always stronger than adverbs or adjectives. Therefore, instead of saying, "Help us to live bravely and courageously, no matter how troubled we may be," say with Robert Louis Stevenson, "Help us to play the man under affliction." Instead of saying: "May we be constantly truthful now in order that ultimately we may live eternally," say with the prayer book: "Grant us in this world knowledge of thy truth; and, in the world to come, life everlasting."

2. *Keep the sentence structure relatively simple:* Remember that, if people are to follow you, they will appreciate short sentences and direct statements rather than the involved tangles of subordinate clauses and the long zigzags of conditional sentences.

3. *Use direct address:* Keep constantly in mind that prayer is a direct approach to God. When it slips into indirect address or when it sinks still deeper into the giving of information which is really addressed to the congregation rather than to God, it ceases to be prayer.

4. *Remember that prayer is akin to poetry:* Poetry has been defined as "the rhythmic emotional expression of significant thought" and public prayer could well be defined as "the rhythmic emotional expression of religious need and aspiration addressed to God in behalf of a worshipping congregation." Therefore prayer, without rhyme or metre should nevertheless use the rhythmic structure, the concrete

and vivid imagery, the emotional coloring which are essentially poetic.

THE COLLECT FORM

How close prayer may be to poetry is revealed by the fact that one form of prayer, the collect, has developed a structure almost as rigid and formal as a sonnet. It will be good discipline for those who lead in public prayer to master the simple collect form and practice writing brief prayers according to this pattern. It consists essentially of the following elements: (1) The Invocation: "Almighty God": (2) The Relative Clause, which indicates the aspect or attribute of God which is in mind: "unto whom all hearts are open, all desires known, and from whom no secrets are hid": (3) The Main Petition: "cleanse the thoughts of our hearts by the inspiration of thy Holy Spirit." (4) The Secondary Petition, which must be definitely related to the main petition only carrying it further, indicating its purpose and giving it deeper meaning: "that we may perfectly love thee and worthily magnify thy holy name." (5) The Ascription: "through Jesus Christ, our Lord. Amen."

THE LITANY

Another form of prayer which has a definite structure though not as close-knit as the collect is the litany. Note in the following beautiful example of this form, written by William H. Spence, the invocation, the cumulative development of thoughts, the rhythmic pattern of sentences and clauses, and the careful choice of beautiful words and phrases which are clear and honest and at the same time resonant with rich overtones of meaning like an old violin.

A LITANY OF PURITY AND GRACE

Almighty God, Spirit of Purity and Grace, whose dwelling is with the humble and contrite heart, hear thy children's confession of sin and grant us thy mercy. For all that has been evil in our lives, for unholy thought and impure motives, for any scorn of goodness, trifling with truth, and indifference to beauty; for all our wanderings from the better way;

Forgive us, O Lord.

For lack of love toward thee whose love has never failed, for doubt of thy goodness and unbelief in thy providence, for ingratitude for blessings received and unwillingness to give of that which thou has given, for any dullness of insight which has kept us unaware of thy glory, and for any disobedience unto such heavenly visions as we have been able to see;

Forgive us, O Lord, and may we henceforth love thee as we ought.

For all the wrong we have done our fellow men; for unkind words and untruthful speech, for loss of temper and irritating conduct, for neglect of charity and failure in justice, for arrogant pride and contempt of the lowly, forgetfulness of others' pain and advantage taken of others' weakness; for whatever any person may rightfully hold against us;

Forgive us, O Lord, and help us to love our neighbor as ourselves.

For our faulty following of the Master, our slow faith in his power to save, our timid, hesitant answers to his call for service, our insensibility to the meaning of his cross; for all that mars our discipleship and makes it difficult for others to believe in him;

Forgive us, O Lord, and give us grace to follow the Master more steadfastly.

Help thy people, our Father, to be truly penitent, empower us to overcome all our temptations, enable us faithfully to live according to thy will, and create within us a growing likeness to Jesus Christ our Lord.

Amen.

THE "BIDDING" PRAYER

Another pattern of prayer which is growing in favor, perhaps more in England than in this country, is what is called the "bidding" prayer. Here information is given not to God but to the worshippers. And on the basis of suggestions made they are invited or "bidden" to make their own prayers silently. The recurring periods of silence make this a peculiarly solemn and restful prayer, a change and relief both from the necessity of following the unexpected twists and turns of even the noblest extempore prayer or, on the other hand, the all too smoothly worn thoroughfare of a prescribed and familiar ritual. Here is a brief pattern illustration of a bidding prayer:

O God, our heavenly Father, who art the Father of Lights, with whom there is no variableness nor shadow that is cast by turning, send out thy light and thy truth. Let them lead us to thy holy hill. Grant to us who live in difficult days of strife and tumult, of actual or threatened war, thy inner peace which the world gave not and the world cannot take away. (Here follows a brief period of silence.) Let us now pray silently and individually for that inward peace amid all the storms of life which has been promised to those who put their trust in God and seek to do his will.

(Here follows a brief period of silence.)

Let us pray for a quiet mind, a fair and discriminating spirit; that, as we have to make decisions in a world filled with the smoke-screens of propaganda and the dust of conflicting interests, we may do so justly and in accordance with God's holy will.

(Here follows a brief period of silence.)

Let us pray for those to whom is entrusted the difficult task of government: that they may be lifted above mere political expediency, shortsighted national selfishness or desire for personal glory, but may be humble, openminded, farsighted, generous, in dealing with all situations where the interests of men and nations clash.

(Here follows a brief period of silence.)

Let us pray for good-will in industry: that all who govern the working conditions of their fellowmen may seek human welfare ahead of selfish personal gain; that the dignity of labor may be recognized; that men who toil may have a just share in determining the conditions under which they work; that no product and no profit may be produced at the cost of injustice, bitterness or human degradation.

(Here follows a brief period of silence.)

Let us pray for world peace: that men may not take the sword lest they perish by the sword and drag all civilization down to the abyss; that the causes and occasions for war may be recognized and justly dealt with in advance; and that patience may replace arrogance, and good-will and fair play govern where suspicion and fear threaten to distort men's judgment.

(Here follows a brief period of silence.)

O God, the God of all peace and concord, of justice and good-will, grant that the words of our mouths and the meditations of our hearts and the deeds of our hands may all combine to praise thee, to do thy holy will and to help toward the building up of thy kingdom of peace and love and justice upon the earth. Through Jesus Christ, our Lord, Amen.

SHALL PRAYERS BE IMPROVISED OR READ?

Shall the minister improvise his prayers upon the impulse of the moment trusting to the deep that calleth unto deep within his own soul; or shall he write them out or plan them out in advance, practically committing them to memory; or shall he write them out and read them; or shall he trust himself to the prayers of others and read or recite from memory the prayers available in great classic liturgies or prepared by men more gifted in the language of devotion than he feels himself to be?

Probably the best answer is that he may wisely employ all of these methods of public prayer at different times according to the occasion and somewhat also according to his own mood and ability. And he had better not be limited to any one of them! Much is to be said for the extempore prayer which is improvised out of the urgency of the moment and comes hot from the volcanic depths of the soul. There is something mysterious about all high art. Whether it be painting or music or poetry or prayer, at its noblest it is an upthrust from the sub-conscious. But, just the same, that does not mean that the artist never works at his task. The joy of the emergence of something from the sub-conscious, not quite what we planned and better than we planned, comes only to those who have fed into the sub-conscious the materials of faithful toil. Not that every plodder will ultimately be inspired, not that, but rather that inspiration will be but an insubstantial and evanescent flame if the fires of the sub-conscious have not been well supplied with fuel.

Applying all this to public prayer, must we not recognize that, while improvised prayer may rise the highest in its power to kindle the emotions of the hearers, it may also fall the lowest? Its consistent strength depends upon hidden sources, chief of which are the spiritual intensity of the minister's own life, his private prayers and his familiarity with the great literature of devotion as expressed in hymns, prayers, and lyric poems.

Because he cannot always be in the mood for extemporaneous prayer, and in order to enrich his own soul and the

souls of his hearers, enlarging their powers of spiritual expression and covering a wide range of needs and interests,
the minister will do well to have at hand and frequently
to use as far as needed, until his own powers of utterance
take wing, some of the noble prayers, ancient and modern,
by which great saints or troubled souls have uttered their
hunger for God. Thus he can be sure that the element of
prayer, which is central in any public worship service, will
not fail any seeker after God who may have come to the
church that day with a hungry soul or a heavy heart or a
deep sense of spiritual longing for more intimate communion with the Most High.

CHAPTER TEN

The Sacraments

EXTREMES MEET! The high Episcopal church, with altar, candles, incense, genuflections, ornate vestments and a rigid ritual, celebrates the Holy Communion, and possibly even calls it Mass, every Sunday. So does the plain austere Disciples church with almost none of the high church symbolism, with a largely extemporized ritual, though rigid enough at certain points, too, and with laymen conducting the service. Only it calls it the Lord's Supper. But, in between the high road and the low, which after all have something in common, the rest drift to and fro! Some denominations hold a communion service once a month, others once in two months, others once a quarter. The simple and somewhat disconcerting fact remains that, with the great majority of American protestants, the sacrament of the Lord's Supper is not universally revered. Many who observe it do so with inadequate appreciation of its meaning or value simply because it is a custom inherited from the past. Some church members actually stay away if they know it is communion Sunday or else heave a sigh when they enter the church and note the white cloth over the communion table. A choice inner circle of worshippers welcome and revere it, however, and only a relatively few iconoclasts would favor giving it up entirely.

And yet this is historically at the very center of Christian worship! What has happened that, in great areas of protestantism, it has so largely lost its centrality, beauty and appeal? Has the sacrament of the Lord's Supper really an abiding and genuine value for modern men? And, if so, how can it be reclaimed and restored to a full and adequate place in Christian worship? How can people be brought to understand its deep significance and thus to welcome it back into their lives and exalt it in the corporate life of the church? Or must we write "Ichabod, the glory has departed," above this ancient sacrament of Christendom? Much will be lost if we do; for, while theories concerning it have driven deep wedges of division into the church of Christ, nevertheless the fact that, in one way or another, in all denominations, the Lord's Supper has been honored and observed has been a great symbolic witness of essential Christian unity.

There are several reasons for the relative unpopularity of the Lord's Supper among some protestants. If the layman could and would speak frankly he might arise and say that, trivial as the objection seems, the Lord's Supper has suffered from the disadvantage that it unduly lengthened the morning service and made people late for Sunday dinner. Others would feel that, as often conducted, it was shadowed with a somber unreality. This was still worse when superstitious fears were aroused by dark and forboding warnings based on St. Paul's cryptic utterance concerning the dangers of partaking unworthily.[1] Still other laymen would say that they were not interested in symbolism, quite unconscious of their deep entanglement in symbolism at their lodges or in business or politics. Yet

[1] I Cor. 11:27-32.

others would say: "There is nothing new in it. It is just the same routine over and over again. I know it all in advance." And, finally, a few might say: "I go to church to get new and stimulating ideas and the communion service simply shortens the sermon or even eliminates it altogether."

Now, since the Lord's Supper is a symbol, let us recognize quite frankly that Christianity might survive without it. Historically it has done so in the case of the Quakers and the Salvation Army. Its value is in its symbolism but that value exists only for those who recognize it and welcome it. When there is passive disregard or active dislike of the Lord's Supper because of some earlier lack of training or unhappy experience, may not the wisest thing to do be simply to find other ways by which the symbolic values of the communion service may be mediated to those who need them? After all, souls are to be saved. Sacraments are valuable only so far as they are valuable, which means only so far as they are welcomed as outward and visible signs of inner and spiritual truths and are received with gratitude and joy.

The Oxford and Edinburgh Conferences in the summer of 1937 illustrated this point admirably though quite unconsciously. Neither conference could hold an official corporate communion service because of divergent sacramental theories and the conscientious scruples of certain members. A communion service was held in each case, however; at Oxford by the Anglicans and at Edinburgh by the Presbyterians, and such as chose to do so attended, while those whose conscientious scruples prevented their joining in stayed away. But did the conferences, therefore, have to do without spiritual food and inspiration? By no

means! In St. Mary's at Oxford and St. Giles' in Edinburgh, there were glorious and uplifting services of worship, conducted by leaders from many denominations and
participated in by all. These services had truly sacramental
values in that, while bread and wine were not physically
present, the love and adoration of Jesus, a high faith in
God and a hushed waiting for the Holy Spirit were present.
Thus, without physical emblems which would have given
offense to some, these great ecumenical conferences
achieved in these simple worship services a sense of spiritual unity which was a large part of the secret of their
success.

Is there not in this a parable and a pattern for the local
church? If part of your congregation or an element in your
community is, for some reason, conditioned against the use
of the sacraments, the problem becomes how to secure for
them in some other way the spiritual values of which the
sacraments are normally the channels. The other thing to
do, and both solutions, of course, ought to be worked out
simultaneously, is to re-educate them as to the nature and
value of sacraments and win them to a happy and unhesi-
tating participation in sacramental worship.

How, then, can we make the communion service more
meaningful and heartily welcomed in the average protestant church?

In some cases might it not help if the sacrament were
made a privilege rather than an imposed routine? I mean
by this to suggest the value of taking it out of the morning
service and making it a separate service at a time set apart
for it and for it alone. This might result in a smaller attendance but a more deeply devotional spirit on the part

of those who did attend. Only those would be there who really wanted to share in the sacrament. There would be no anxiety over an undue lengthening of the service, or a shortening or omission of the sermon, and there would be no hurry but rather an ample opportunity to exemplify and develop the worshipful values of the occasion in a sympathetic atmosphere. Word as to the impressiveness and helpfulness of such a service would spread, attendance would grow and appreciation deepen. The best time for such a service might well be in the evening. While there is ample historical evidence and continued practice of early morning communion down through the Christian centuries, we may also remember that its earliest observance and the last supper of Jesus himself with the disciples were at night. The best way to begin in many churches might be to announce such a service for the evening of Holy Thursday—the very night in Holy Week on which Jesus ate the supper with his disciples. Other evening celebrations might well be on Ash Wednesday, at the beginning of Lent, or on New Year's Eve. If and when the sacrament is to be observed on Sunday morning, it should be no mere additional item or afterthought in an already overcrowded hour. Rather, ought it not to be announced in advance and made the central feature of the service? In this way those not interested could stay away or go elsewhere; while, for those who came, there would need be no extension of the service beyond its usual time limits. It would simply be a different type of service, exalted and welcomed for its own sake.

How to make the Lord's Supper loved and welcomed is, therefore, the real problem in many an American church.

Two things are necessary to this end; first, that it should
be understood; and, second, that, when celebrated, it should
be done with such dignity, simple beauty and rich content
of meaning that the worshippers would find it ministering
to their spiritual needs and thus rejoice in it and come to
look forward to its recurrence.

How may the Lord's Supper be better understood? The
process of education or re-education may well start in the
pastor's class preparatory to church membership, and it
may also be continued in Lenten lectures for adults on the
ways and means of spiritual living and by an occasional
sermon, or even passing references in many sermons. We
also need a good brief book giving the history, meaning
and values of the Lord's Supper, which could be circulated
among the more thoughtful people in the churches.

But the best education will come to people by actual
participation in a beautiful and reverently conducted service of Holy Communion itself. Let us therefore ask ourselves what are the essentials of such an observance. Brilioth, a contemporary Swedish theologian, suggests that
there are five elements to be considered and given their
due place in the communion service:

1. Commemoration or Memorial.
2. Thanksgiving.
3. Fellowship or Communion.
4. Sacrifice.
5. Mystery.

While this stimulating analysis of the different elements
in the sacrament is capable of almost indefinite expansion,
it also has the value of compactness. The whole meaning
is here and can be translated into very simple language

and procedure. To illustrate this let me submit the use I made of these five points when called upon to conduct the sacrament at a young people's retreat in the large common room of a country-club after a program which had included both outdoor sports and serious discussion of religious problems. There was no choir, no pulpit, no vestments, no traditional ecclesiastical setting whatever—just a table with the elements reverently placed upon it, two candles, lights dimmed and a little group of singers near the piano ready to lead out in appropriate hymns at times agreed upon but without announcement. After a hymn, "Sun of my soul, thou Savior dear," and a brief scripture reading and invocation, I called attention to Brilioth's five points and suggested that we follow them in our meditation as we sat together around the table of our Lord. Then I spoke somewhat as follows:

"The first word in our understanding of the Lord's Supper is Commemoration. This sacred act is rooted in history. Our thoughts go back to an historic event tonight. We are thinking of Jesus and the twelve in the upper room. We remember their peril, their distress of mind and also the things that Jesus did and said, how he washed their feet as an example of humble brotherly service, spoke to them great words of peace and reassurance, and gave to them the bread and wine of this sacrament." Here the group by the piano led out in singing, without announcement, "Fairest Lord Jesus."

Then I proceeded: "The second word is Thanksgiving. In some churches the Lord's Supper is spoken of as the Eucharist, and that is a very ancient name which means the giving of thanks. We read in the Gospels how 'Jesus took the cup and gave thanks,' even though it was the symbol of his outpoured blood. Let us pause for silent meditation on the things or people for whose presence in our lives we would ourselves give thanks." After a period of silence, the group near the piano led all of us in singing, "Break thou the bread of life, dear Lord to me."

"The third word is Fellowship. It was a group that gathered in that upper room. Where two or three are gathered together in the Master's spirit, there the promised blessing comes. But we cannot limit our fellowship to just the little company of friends and sympathetic minds here. We belong to all humanity. Like John Wesley, we have taken the world for our parish. Let us pause in silence to forgive if any have wronged us, and to pray for world-wide Christian fellowship and human brotherhood." And again, after the period of silence, the singers led in singing, "In Christ there is no east, or west."

"Our fourth word is Sacrifice. This sacrament was instituted almost within the shadow of the cross. Jesus was consciously laying down his life. He made the bread and wine the symbols of his broken body and sacrificial death. But Jesus cannot do it all. The world will only be saved at last by saviours, people who are willing to labor, to suffer, to endure hardship, to face death, if necessary, that peace and good-will, righteousness and truth, may live. This sacrament invites us all to consecrate ourselves in sacrificial devotion to something greater than ourselves." Again a period of silence, followed by singing, "When I survey the wondrous cross."

"The fifth word is Mystery. Christianity grew up amid the so-called mystery religions of the Graeco-Roman world.

It had also its great mystery, which was symbolized in this sacrament, the mystery of God above and beyond the evil and suffering of the present age and revealed to men in the beautiful human life and sacrificial death of Jesus Christ. Life is not easy. It has its shadows, its struggles, its seeming defeats. There are vast depths in the universe we do not understand. But our Christian faith is that, at the heart of all mystery, there is, at the last, the goodness of God as revealed in Jesus Christ and ultimately that, and that alone, shall triumph. Let us trust ourselves in silent prayer to that God of all the universe whose everlasting arms are underneath us and who has promised never to leave us or forsake us." And again the verse of a hymn followed the silent prayer, "O God, our help in ages past." Next came the "comfortable words":

"Hear what comfortable words our Saviour Christ saith unto all who truly turn to him: Come unto me all ye that labor and are heavy laden and I will give you rest . . . I am come that ye might have life and have it abundantly."

Being now in a mood to receive the sacrament, the service proceeded with the call to communion: "Therefore, ye that do earnestly repent of your sins and are in love and charity with your neighbors, and intend to lead a new life, following the commandments of God and walking from henceforth in his holy ways, draw near with faith and take this holy sacrament to your comfort; and devoutly make your humble confession unto almighty God."

This prepared for the prayer of humble access: "We do not presume to come to this thy table, O merciful Lord, trusting in our own righteousness, but in thy manifold and great mercies. We are not worthy so much as to gather up the crumbs under thy table, but thou art the same Lord, whose mercy is unfailing. Grant us, therefore, gracious Lord, so to partake of these memorials of thy Son Jesus Christ, that we may be filled with the fullness of his life, may grow into his likeness and may evermore dwell in him, and he in us. Amen."

Following this came the simple "words of institution," quoted from St. Paul, the prayer of consecration and the distribution of the bread and then of the individual communion cups, by those appointed to serve as deacons. Then the post-communion verses: "I am the vine, ye are the branches" . . ., the closing hymn, "Christ for the world we sing," and the benediction.

I have not quoted this experience of a very informal communion service, conducted without hymn books or even a mimeographed order of service, because it is in all respects a model. Indeed, some readers with liturgical learning and more conventional preferences may find themselves distinctly shocked at the dislocations of traditional order and free use of material which it exhibits. The point is precisely that such material can be used freely, provided a genuine spiritual experience is achieved.

Here is another brief order of worship which was used at an early morning communion service held in the chancel of the University of Chicago chapel for a group of attendants at a pastors' institute. It is very brief, taking only a half-hour including the serving of the communion, and there is no sermon. This service, incidentally, also illustrates several points which have been emphasized in this book, notably the arrangement of the responsive reading so that the part taken by the congregation is in each case a real response to what the leader has just read, and also the use of a brief confession of faith said in unison. Brilioth's elements of Commemoration, Thanksgiving, Fellowship, Sacrifice and Mystery also are all here.

AN EARLY MORNING COMMUNION SERVICE

Organ Prelude and Meditation.
Hymn: "Light of the World, we hail thee."
Call to Worship.

> *Minister:* We are children of the sunrise and the morning gathered here as followers of Him who with the fewest hours accomplished Thy divinest work.
>
> *People:* O Lord, send out thy light and thy truth, let them lead us to thy holy hill.
>
> *Minister:* We have come into this our upper room in devout and loving memory of the Master who, one shadowed evening in the long ago, gave to his disciples the symbols of the holy grail and broken bread.
>
> *People:* O Thou who makest the out-goings of the morning and the evening to rejoice, keep us in thy love this day and for-ever more.
>
> *Minister:* In company with all our fellow pilgrims of the spiritual life, and in the face of all the turmoil and difficulty of our days, we confess our faith in things unseen and yet eternal and our abiding hope in goodness, truth and beauty.
>
> *All:* We believe in the fatherhood of God and in the brotherhood of man. We believe that Christ is the way and the truth and the life. We believe in the clean heart and the unworldly life, and in the service of love that Jesus exemplified. We accept his spirit and his teaching and dedicate ourselves to his unfinished work. Amen.

Hymn: "Dear Lord and Father of Mankind."

> *Minister:* Hear what comfortable words our Savior Christ saith unto all that truly turn to him: "Come unto me, all ye that labor and are heavy laden and I will give you rest." "If any

man hear my voice and open the door, I will come in to him and will sup with him." Therefore lift up your hearts with peace and joy.

People: We lift them up unto the Lord.

Minister: Let us give thanks unto the Lord.

People: It is meet and right so to do.

Minister: For thy presence within us, O God, and for this sacrament of remembrance of Jesus the true and living way, we give thee thanks.

People: We do not presume to come to this thy table, O merciful Lord, trusting in our own righteousness but in thy manifold and great mercies. Grant us, therefore, so to partake of this sacrament of thy dear Son that our souls may be made clean and that we may evermore dwell in him and he in us. Amen.

The Words of Institution.

The Blessing and Administration of the Bread and of the Cup.

Hymn: "Rise up, O men of God."

Benediction.

The Lord's Supper, thus conducted, while filled with dignity and true solemnity, is not depressing. Nor is it removed from reality or the living issues of the age in which we live. It should rather be a source of deep courage and high resolve, binding us together in a glorious fellowship with Christ and all who have sought to follow him across the centuries. Such a service keeps the church conscious of its deep historic rootage in the life and character of Jesus. It says in a language of symbols some things of which we need constantly to be reminded. And it leaves open the door for personal worship and private meditation and encourages people to invite their own souls on the high quest of communion with God.

As in the case of anything really worth doing, there are

details which need to be cared for. All announcements of the various items in the service should of course be carefully avoided so that the spiritual experience of the hour shall flow like a river. If the order of service is printed or mimeographed, it should be, if possible, on paper the same size as the hymn-book pages so as to be more easily handled.

The pews, in churches where the deacons serve the seated congregation, should be equipped with noiseless holders for the empty communion cups. The practice, prevalent in some places, of having the congregation retain the bread, and later the cup, until all have been served and then all partaking together, is of questionable value. It seems too reminiscent of drinking a toast, and the communion is not that, but the deeper objection is that there is something very personal about taking communion which is lost by this regimented wholesale participation. Communion is an act of fellowship, but it is also an act of personal worship and dedication. There is something very impressive about the way in which people take communion together and yet alone, each receiving his own morsel of bread and his miniature cup and eating or drinking it alone, with his own individual prayers and meditations and yet in the presence of many others doing the same thing. Should the organ play during the distribution of the elements? If at all, very softly and only old hymns or very subdued and familiar religious music which will not be in any way obtrusive. But I wonder if, after all, absolute silence at such a time is not more impressive than any music possibly can be?

Should the minister at the Lord's Supper stand facing the people across the table or should he stand with his back to the people, facing the table as though it were an altar? Even if the table really is an altar back against the wall of the chancel, as is becoming more common, the instinct of a protestant minister of the puritan tradition will be to face the people. He may, therefore, prefer to stand at one side of the altar in conducting the liturgy, only turning his back to the congregation when he takes the bread or the communion cups from the altar and then standing holding them in his hands and facing the congregation as he says: "Jesus said unto them: This is my body which is broken for you. This do in remembrance of me. Ministering in his name, I give you this bread;" or "This cup is the new covenant in my blood. This do, as oft as ye drink it, in remembrance of me. Ministering in his name, I give you this cup." Respect and honor are due to the altar on which stands the cross of Christ and from which his supper is served, but we also need to remember the penetrating word of Bishop Moule of Durham that Christ is "present not *on* the Holy Table but *at* it." The real presence of Christ in which protestants believe is not anything that can be localized on the altar, but is a much more mystical presence in the hearts of the congregation wherever they seek to worship in spirit and in truth. "Where two or three are gathered together in my name, there am I . . . Lo, I am with you alway, even unto the end of the world."

In order to avoid the question as to whether one should face the altar or the congregation, and also because of the value of going back to a far earlier and simpler symbolism, much may be said in favor of a communion table which is a real table, standing in the midst of the chancel and clear of the wall so that the minister may stand behind it with his deacons grouped around on either side. Such an arrangement makes it perfectly clear that what is taking place is not a medieval or modern Catholic mass, by which a miracle is being wrought upon the altar, but a primitive Christian or protestant celebration of the Lord's Supper, by which all who love the Lord Jesus in sincerity and truth are invited to gather about the table of the Lord even as did the little band of the disciples in the upper room.

It is assumed that individual communion cups will, of course, be used: but there is no reason why a large silver flagon and one or two silver cups or chalices should not stand upon the table for their symbolic value. If there is a cross on the table that will need to be removed, since the minister will not want to stand with it between him and the people. It can be placed on a shelf back of and higher than the table at communion services, or, if there is a curtain behind the table, the cross may be placed back against the curtain on a special pedestal high enough to lift it above the heads of those serving at the table. Thus the cross looks down upon the scene and brings an added touch of symbolism.

Preparation for the communion has long been a tradition in the Christian church. The Roman Catholic prepares for it by making his confession and receiving absolution, and the puritan protestant by attending a preparatory service. Many a Scotch story refers to the "tokens" given to those who attended the preparatory service which entitled them to participate in the communion on the Sabbath. In these strenuous and complicated days, however, the preparatory service has largely faded out. What then? Shall the worshipper make no preparation for the sacrament? May it not be that this preparation will best be personal and individual and how to make it may well be one of the points on which careful and definite instruction ought to be given to all before they take their first communion?

An interesting plan for such a personal preparation would include scripture to be read, like the ten commandments and the 13th chapter of First Corinthians, together with searching personal questions to be meditated upon. The heart of the matter and the scope and range of the preparation desirable before partaking of the Lord's Supper is admirably and compactly set forth in the following call to communion in the prayer-book: "Ye that do truly and earnestly repent of your sins, and are in love and charity with your neighbors, and intend to lead a new life, following the commandments of God, and walking from henceforth in his holy ways, draw near with faith, and take this holy sacrament to your comfort; and devoutly make your humble confession to Almighty God." This is a searching and soul-stirring summary of the great loyalties of the Christian life. He who examines himself objectively along these lines will be his own father confessor, and will approach the sacrament in humility and reverence. It has been suggested recently that church members ought to renew their vows every year. Such an invitation to communion as is given above would make every Lord's Supper a renewal of consecration to the Christian life and its essential attitudes; and that is just what the Communion service ought to be.

Baptism also is a part of the worship experience of the Christian church. Since it occurs but once in each individual's lifetime and, is a symbol of cleansing from sin and consecration to the Christian way of living and of entrance into the fellowship of believers, it ought, obviously, to be beautiful and dignified in its liturgical setting. For churches which use immersion, the First Baptist Church of Evanston, Illinois, has an admirable arrangement. There is a chancel with a communion table, behind which is a great curtain of deep red, high against which hangs a golden cross. When baptism takes place, the lower portion of this curtain is parted, disclosing the baptistry, below the cross and just above the communion table. This keeps the baptistry central when in use and surrounds it with appropriate symbolism. In churches which baptize by sprinkling the location of the font is always a problem. Ideally it should be in a separate chapel or baptismal alcove near the door of the church, thus symbolizing baptism as the entrance into the Christian fellowship. In churches where there is a deep-rooted custom of presenting babies for baptism at Easter, Christmas, Children's Day and other stated occasions practical necessity dictates a location at the front of the church, usually on the floor of the nave near the lectern.

In the christening of little children it is important to combine reasonable brevity with a liturgical setting which shall make clear the meaning and purpose of the act. The father and mother and sponsors, if there are to be sponsors, should be escorted to the font by one of the deacons. The minister meets them there, the choir meanwhile singing some hymn appropriate to childhood such as "I think when I read that sweet story of old" or "By cool Siloam's shady rill." The minister may then quote appropriate scripture verses concerning childhood, especially Jesus' regard for little children, and then address the parents and spon-

sors somewhat as follows: "My dear friends, in bringing
this little child for Christian baptism, you are performing
toward him one of the sacred duties of fatherhood and
motherhood. By this ancient symbolic act which has come
down to us across the centuries you seek to express your
faith that this little one is not only your child but God's
child, and your desire to dedicate him to God, looking forward to the day when he shall confirm this act of dedication
in his behalf by entering into full and gladly chosen membership in the Christian church. You, therefore, as parents
(and sponsors), promise to bring this child up in the nur-
ture and admonition of the Lord, teaching him to pray and
read the Bible, and doing all in your power that he may
grow up to be a strong and useful Christian man. You so
covenant?" Response: "We do." (Feminine pronoun will,
of course, be used if the child is a girl or plurals if more
than one child is being presented for baptism.)

Here may follow the prayer, which should be brief but
comprehensive and may follow along these lines: "O God,
our Heavenly Father, whose promise is to us and to our
children, we thank thee for the constant renewal of life
through the coming of little children into the world. Keep,
guard and bless this child. May he be a bringer of joy to
the home and, as he grows in years, may he also grow in
wisdom and favor with God and man, through the knowledge and grace of our Lord Jesus Christ. Lead his feet out
into paths of service, teach his hands to do the deeds that
upbuild the world and may the law of kindness be upon his
tongue. Bless also these parents (and sponsors) in their
care of this little child. Grant that this home may be an
abode of peace and joy, a place where thy honor dwelleth.

So may the Spirit of Jesus rest upon this child and this home now and evermore. Amen."

Then the minister, first asking, "What name shall be given to this child?" will baptize the child, saying: "N——, I baptize thee in the name of the Father and of the Son and of the Holy Spirit. The Lord bless you and keep you. Amen."

Following this, a simple benediction by the minister such as, "Go in peace; the Lord be with you," and the baptismal party is escorted out by the deacon, the choir meanwhile singing an appropriate hymn such as "Savior, like a shepherd lead us." At a home christening, the procedure will be much the same, except that there will probably be no choir to sing. In some churches the deacon gives each child a flower after its baptism. This usually pleases the child and adds an innocent touch of sentiment. Should the minister take the child in his arms? Children are usually happy at a christening, being interested in the music and the scene; but, since at certain ages particularly, they may be fearful of strangers it is wiser for the minister to let the father continue holding the child. For the same reason it is better to defer the actual baptism until near the close of the ceremony since some children are apt to be alarmed by the hand of the minister touching them. In the christening service just outlined, however, it will be noted that the child is disturbed as little as possible, hoping that the vows and prayers will be better heard and more impressive than when said to the accompaniment of a child's crying.

Adult baptism sometimes presents a problem because of occasional diffidence, particularly in the case of men. Men are apt to dread undergoing it before a congregation.

In as much as the value of adult baptism lies in its contribution to the inner life of the person being baptized, the minister can suggest a private baptism, with no one else present, or only such members of the immediate family as are requested. Such a service can then be made a very intimate and personal act of dedication, far more meaningful because of the absence of self-consciousness and a certain man to man relationship which it establishes with the officiating minister.

CHAPTER ELEVEN

Worship and the Social Gospel

Is WORSHIP MERELY AN ESCAPE MECHANISM? In highly sophisticated circles it is sometimes dismissed from serious consideration as just another form of self-deception built up by the mind to cushion itself against the shocks of reality. It is assumed, therefore, that, when once this is realized, tough-minded and superior persons will have no further personal concern about worship except as a popular psychological fantasy. They may condescendingly admit that it has, perhaps, some value in soothing the minds of simple unlearned folk but feel that it is bound to disappear among the informed and critical. The educated and sophisticated could, therefore, dismiss it from serious consideration were it not for the danger that, like all narcotic drugs, worship may be wrongly used to lull to indifference or unconsciousness the social progress of the race. Defeated in their efforts here, and finding the Kingdom of God hard to realize on earth, may not people take refuge in other-worldliness and satisfy their social hungers by merely praying about the better social order which they have failed actually to achieve?

The answer to this very modern objection to worship is that it grows out of an imperfect understanding of worship, a failure to discriminate between different kinds of escape and their possible values, and an almost complete blindness

to the power worship has of releasing dynamic social idealism. Let us take these points up and look at them more
carefully.

1. *Is Worship Just Other-Worldliness?*

That some worship may be only an escape into another
world, a compensation for the troubles of this life by running away from them, may sometimes be true. There are
services of worship and forms of liturgy which seem to have
no contact with the actual world, but they are relatively the
exception. For the most part people attend worship in order
that they may gain strength and refreshment for living. A
good service of worship, as we have seen, will have in it an
element of re-dedication. The committal which it seeks is
not just a passive submission to God, but a consecration to
do the will of God here in this present world. Worship of
the purely passive sort is decidedly exceptional. Monks in
their secluded cells, shut off from the world and its needs,
may worship in a way that has no contact with reality, but
normal men and women, facing life's daily problems, go
to church that they may gain either a new vision or a rein-
forcement of faith and courage which will enable them to
take up life's duties more effectively.

Worship is other-worldly only in the sense that a steamship line is European. The steamship line takes Americans
to Europe, of course. But not many of them stay there
permanently. It brings them back again, and sometimes
Europeans with them. And such Americans return with
deeper insights, cultural, artistic, religious. They see their
own country through new lenses. American advantages are
more cherished and appreciated after a trip to Europe, but

also, if one is openminded and objective, certain American limitations and shortcomings are also more clearly recognized. On the basis of such an experience, the normal person ought to be a better citizen, with wider horizons of sympathy and a better standard of values.

So worship, in a sense, is other-worldly, but the question is: Does it just leave people in that other world or does it bring them home again? And when they come home, what has happened to them? Are they just homesick for heaven, as some Americans seem to be homesick for Europe? In a few cases, yes. But in most cases the result is by no means so paralyzing to social usefulness. Most of the great reforms have been started not by secularists but by men and women who found in worship a normal replenishment of insight, energy and courage. Everything depends upon the kind of a God men seek, and find, in that other world!

2. *Is Escape Always Bad?*

Even if worship were purely an escape from present troubles, would it be undesirable or worthless? In a world of tension, such as we live in, is not escape absolutely necessary? Ought we not, indeed, to welcome escapes that are innocent or constructive, and denounce only these that undermine life and cost too high a price in physical, mental or moral deterioration. Alcohol, gambling, watching a prize fight, attending a football game or a movie or a play, or a symphony concert, playing a musical instrument, going to Europe, reading a good book, sleep, conversation with friends, building a new house, a vacation, marching in a parade, signing a petition for peace or better housing or racial justice, going to church, worship, prayer: all of these are escapes. Surely one must learn to discriminate between them!

Suppose worship had no contribution to make to practical problems beyond quieting the soul and smoothing down life's ruffled feathers, it would still be worthy of approval. We should count it, then, akin to music or any other art which rests us by transferring our attention for a little while to an ideal world where harmony and beauty prevail. When one contemplates the perils of alcohol and gambling to which so many people turn for escape when life becomes too much for them, we surely ought to welcome and encourage almost any innocent diversion, like worship, which can bring relief from the over-tenseness of life without paralyzing the brain, breaking down the body, disintegrating personal morale or destroying habits of thrift and industry. But, of course, worship is not just pure escape. Not even music is that, or any other art. Every art, and worship most of all, has creative power and releases new energies as well as giving rest and refreshment to old ones.

3. *Worship as Release of Energy*

How worship releases new energy we do not fully know, but certainly it is partly due to the contemplation of the ideal as is the case in all great art. One comes back from a study and better understanding, or even just the effortless contemplation, of music or architecture or painting or drama or landscape gardening or any other art with a new sensitivity to ugliness and disharmony and a quickened desire to do something about it.

If there is nothing one can do in the real world round about, the mind takes refuge in a world of phantasy. In the realm of social ideals, this has resulted in the creation of great imaginative works like Bunyan's *Pilgrim's Progress*, Milton's *Paradise Lost*, More's *Utopia*, Dante's *Divine Comedy*, Plato's *Republic*, the *Book of Revelation*, the *Book of Daniel*. Denied the opportunity to walk the ways of earth, the social dream takes wings and dwells in the land of eternal sunrise which is the inspired imagination. Bunyan was in prison, Milton was blind and defeated, Thomas More was confronted by Cardinal Wolsey and Henry VIII, Dante an exile, Plato face to face with petty Greek politics and the authors of Revelation and Daniel suffering persecution. But what they wrote was not mere escape, not just a running away from reality. It had survival value. It is the way the social dream persists in the face of frustration and temporary defeat. If we should in our day enter an age of world-wide dictators and the church had to retreat into the catacombs of a purely personal religion, the social ideal would still survive and find some form of expression beyond the reach of persecution, censorship and propaganda.

But here in America today we do not face the blank walls of defeat which frustrated the men just mentioned. We still live in a land of relative freedom and opportunity for social reconstruction. Into our worship we can weave the social dream. We can pray for world peace, industrial righteousness and inter-racial good-will. We can lift up before God our ideal of civil liberty, of alabaster cities undimmed by human tears, of decent housing for the humblest workers, of health and education for all, in the very language of our worship services. And when we do so, who can tell what a release of energy, what new dynamic of devotion may issue forth to the creation of a better social order?

One vital question facing every minister today, therefore, is not only how to preach the social gospel but how to weave it into the warp and woof of Christian worship. Dr. Charles Clayton Morrison, editor of the "Christian Century" and author of *The Social Gospel and the Christian Cultus* has well pointed out that no great reform comes by preaching alone. Only as nobler social ideals and higher standards of business morality, international dealings and inter-racial respect find their place in the sanctuary of Christian worship will they become completely and unquestionably a part of the church's message to the world. We are much more apt to take positive, determined and continuous action concerning the things we pray about than we are concerning the things about which other people talk to us, no matter how eloquently.

This whole matter was boldly and admirably dealt with by the Oxford Conference on Church, State and Community in 1937. Ringing words like these should not be allowed to slumber unacted-upon in a printed report:

The supreme duty of the churches in all countries as they face the present situation in the world of states and nations is to repent before God, not only by corporate acts of repentance, but by awakening the spirit of repentance in all their members: repentance for things done and things left undone. Judgment must begin at the House of God. If as Christians we are deeply disquieted by the political development of our age and our time, we have to acknowledge a large share of responsibility. We have not lived up to the word of our Lord. "Ye are the salt of the earth and the light of the world." We have not expressed our faith in the redeeming cross of Christ in terms of social relations. We have accepted with-

out clear protest existing social divisions. In like manner we recognize that churches have at times substituted for the true totali-
tarianism of Christ, which requires that every activity and every
relation should be subject to the will of God, a forced totalitarian-
ism, political in character. They have too often been far more
concerned for their own security and prestige in this world than
for fulfilling their Lord's commission and serving mankind in the
spirit of self-sacrificing love. We today acknowledge with deep
humility our share in that guilt.

With repentance must go reconsecration. Penitence, if sincere,
must bear fruit in action. We therefore resolve by God's grace to
do our utmost to prevent the repetition of such sins in the future;
to discharge our duties as citizens in the spirit of Christian love;
and, so far as in us lies, to create a spirit which will enable the
State to fulfil its God-given task of maintaining justice and ministering to the welfare of the people.[1]

One of the tasks laid upon the church, which it is not easy to
carry out in the existing state of things, is to reestablish in the experience of men and women a unity of work and worship. While
their irrelevance to one another at the present time is partly because much work is pagan and unworshipful, it is also due to the
fact that the daily business of the modern world, and the problems
and issues dealt with in this report, are not sufficiently woven into
the liturgy and worship of the church. Unless men are required to
ask forgiveness, to make petitions and to give thanks for the things
with which they are chiefly concerned day by day, public worship
will begin to seem secondary. There should be no discontinuity
between the sanctuary and the life and work in office, factory or
home, for the God we worship cares for the whole of men's life,
and not only for that part of it which is specifically religious.[2]

Here in America a great beginning has been made toward a liturgical expression of Christian social ideals by

[1] *Op. cit.*, p. 27.
[2] *The Messages and Decisions of the Oxford Conference on Church, Community and State*, p. 52.

Walter Rauschenbusch in his *Prayers of the Social Awakening*. This collection of prayers filled with social sympathy and aspiration is coming into ever larger use and inspired by it an increasing number of prayers and litanies, and also poems capable of use in worship services, are making their appearance. As an illustration of the use which can be made of contemporaneous material, here is a service of worship composed largely of quotations from the Oxford Conference and prepared for use at an annual meeting of the International Council of Religious Education.

THE CHURCH AND SOCIAL IDEALS

Prelude.

Scripture Reading.

Invocation.

Hymn: "Rise Up, O Men of God." Tune: St. Thomas.

A Litany of Social Faith and Ideals.

Minister: The Christian Church is called upon to fulfil its mission today amidst a distraught and disunited mankind. Traditional pieties and loyalties and standards of conduct have lost their unquestioned authority. In many countries vigorous attempts are being made to restore social unity by drastic control and regimentation and by making national or class unity the supreme good. In the midst of such a world, torn and disrupted, and feverishly seeking a way out of its troubles, the Church of Jesus Christ has to teach its message and fulfil its task.

People: Give us grace, O Lord, to bear a faithful witness in the troubled age in which we live.

Minister: The life of the Church is deeply infected with the very ills from which humanity suffers. The divisions and the conflicts of mankind have been reproduced and even justified within its own borders. The Church's recall of the world to the feet of Christ must be preceded by the recall of itself. The

Church is under call to confess its sin and to seek anew from God forgiveness and the cleansing of its life.

People: We humbly confess our sins and shortcomings as members of the Christian Church and pray for pardon, cleansing and renewal.

Minister: Persons of all races should become, to the Christian, sons and daughters of God, differing in color, in native endowment, in custom and outlook, but of one brotherhood in God's love and so, by God's grace, in the affection of the Christian. It is a standing rebuke to Christians that this attitude has in fact been more fully realized in some secular and non-Christian movements than within the churches. It is a first responsibility of the Christian Church to demonstrate within its own fellowship the reality of community as God intends it. It is commissioned to call all men into the Church, into a divine society that transcends all national and racial limitations and divisions. In its services of public worship, in its more informal fellowship and in its organization, there can be no place or any pretext whatever for exclusion or compulsory segregation because of race or color.

People: Make us truly Christian, O Lord, in all our thoughts and attitudes toward other races.

Minister: In the next decade those who are responsible for guiding the life of the Church must seek to bring under moral control the attitude of their members in economic relationships—just as they have always sought to bring under moral control the attitude of their members in direct personal relationships. This task will involve far more than preaching. It must become an integral part of the whole life and atmosphere of the Church. The Church as a worshiping community must relate its acts of repentance and dedication to the economic order in which its members live. Emphasis must here be placed upon the importance of teaching children and young people before the crusts formed by class and convention close their minds.

People: Incline our hearts, O Lord, toward social and economic justice and deliver us from all class prejudice or blindness.

Minister: The Church is a supra-national fellowship. She draws her members from all nations, and believes that Christ and the Christian heritage are of greater worth than is any national inheritance apart from him. Where she is true to her nature she cannot allow national interests to be set before those of humanity, nor permit any people to fancy that it can develop its national life without a just regard for every other people. She must educate her people to consider themselves as belonging first to God and to his Church, and secondarily to their nation.

People: O God of all the nations, help us to keep our nation in the paths of thine eternal and universal truth.

Minister: Ignorance of what the Christian faith is and of the obligations which it imposes is widespread and alarming, particularly among young people. Still more so is the degree to which Church members fail to take seriously in their business and civic and other social relations the Christian loyalty which they acknowledge. The majority of them seem pathetically ignorant of the Christian way, and of the resources for following it to be had in that communion with God which is the life of the Church. Preaching needs to be supplemented by a full and carefully planned program of Christian education.

People: Help us, O Lord, winsomely to teach the Christian faith in all its larger and deeper meanings.

Minister: Wars, the occasions of war, and all situations which conceal the fact of conflict under the guise of outward peace, are marks of a world to which the Church is charged to proclaim the Gospel of redemption. War involves compulsory enmity, diabolical outrage against human personality, and a wanton distortion of the truth.

People: Deliver us from war, O Lord, and lead us in the ways of just and lasting peace.

Hymn: "Thou Whose Almighty Word." Tune: Italian Hymn.

Benediction.

Following Oxford came the Edinburgh Conference on Faith and Order which was concerned with the problem of how to set forward the cause of Christian unity. This is of very definite importance for the social gospel because the witness of a united and cooperating group of churches will be much more impressive on the outside world than would the voice of any one denomination speaking alone. Reference is made elsewhere in this book to the important part the corporate services of worship had in creating the spirit of mutual trust and understanding both at Oxford and at Edinburgh. It may not be amiss therefore to note that, while recognizing the deep cleavage between Christians on matters like ministerial orders and the sacraments, the Edinburgh report does contain this significant observation: "In non-sacramental worship of God the Father, Son and Holy Spirit, we are agreed that there is little remaining occasion for maintaining the existing divisions between our churches and much common ground already exists for further unity. We are all united in common prayer, which may be expressed in the spoken word, through silence, or by the employment of the sacred treasures of Christian literature, art and music. In this worship we all stand before God in adoration of his majesty, bringing to him our own needs and the needs of our fellow. We wait for his grace in the forgiveness of our sins and for the restoration of our spirits through renewed communion with him, and we dedicate ourselves to his service and the service of all mankind." [3]

And, in the final Affirmation of Unity adopted, *nemine contradicende*, as the solemn closing act of the Edinburgh conference, occur these words: "In this Conference we may gratefully claim that the Spirit of God has made us willing

[3] Report of Second World Conference on Faith and Order, p. 32.

to learn from one another, and has given us a fuller vision of the truth and enriched our spiritual experience. We have lifted up our hearts together in prayer; we have sung the same hymns; together we have read the same Holy Scriptures. We recognize in one another, across the barriers of our separation, a common Christian outlook and a common standard of values. We are therefore assured of a unity deeper than our divisions." [4]

Now these words from Oxford and Edinburgh are worth careful consideration because they are the considered utterances of great ecumenical bodies in which practically all of non-Roman Catholic Christendom was represented. Delegates came from forty countries and one hundred nineteen different ecclesiastical bodies. Their words are not an *ex parte* utterance by a specialized group of social enthusiasts, they are not merely an expression of American activism or modernistic bias. They represent, as nearly as it is possible to secure it today, a cross-section of intelligent, responsible, world-wide Christian opinion.

This, then, is the growing edge of worship today! How to incorporate the awakening social conscience and its deep rootage in Christian ideals into the prayers and litanies, the hymns and confessions of faith, of the living church of of our day is one of the most challenging tasks before the leader of public worship. In proportion as it is done with literary power and liturgical insight will the criticism that worship is just an escape from reality become completely untenable. And who can tell what new social insight, enthusiasm and unconquerable power for human betterment such a rounding out of Christian worship on the side of its social implications may bring?

[4] *Ibid.*, p. 52.

CHAPTER TWELVE

Services for Various Occasions

THE CONDUCT OF SPECIAL SERVICES on various occasions presents an admirable opportunity for the minister to reach people with the message of the Gospel who might never attend the more routine services of his church. At weddings and funerals, at dedications, union thanksgiving services, at a preaching mission or a civic celebration, he has an opportunity greatly to extend his ministry to the unchurched. If his conduct of these services, or only a minor participation in them, is marked by dignity and reverence he may win the attention and turn the thoughts of even the alienated and the secularized toward a greater appreciation of religion and the part it ought to play in life. If, on the other hand, he approaches such opportunities with inadequate preparation, or conducts them in a purely routine manner, tinged with professionalism, flippancy or boredom, or if he sets a price upon such services and counts on them as a source of income, then he has not only lost an opportunity to reach the unchurched but has actually dishonored his calling and discredited the church he serves.

First among these special occasions, and most numerous of them all, are the countless requests to open some public meeting with prayer or close it with a benediction or say grace at some public dinner. How disappointing it is to all well-wishers for religion if they feel that the minister is ill prepared and unequal to the occasion. He hesitates about what to say, obviously improvising as he goes along, or else, with a superficial fluency, he rattles off glib formulas and cant phrases which never get below the surface. Or else he reads something from his prayer-book that is so formal and remote from the heart of the occasion that his participation becomes only a perfunctory bow of recognition toward religion rather than any real lifting of the minds of those present into a sense of the eternal verities.

Every well-trained minister ought to be able to say grace with brevity and yet in such a way that everyone in the room has a feeling of hushed recognition of God as the great giver of all good things and a sense of reverent awe for the blessings of life. If you have ever seen that rollicking, wholesome comedy "You Can't Take It With You," you know how moving a very unconventional blessing said at table can be. Personally I shall never forget the blessing at her meager meal for orphan boys which I once heard a great actress say in a play the very name of which I have forgotten. Did the minister really thank God for something and help us all to a humbler and more grateful attitude of mind or did he just mumble off a routine formula? That is a test which, consciously or unconsciously, all the people in the room are making. If they feel the genuineness of your gratitude, you may have awakened and helped them toward a more spiritual appreciation for all of life's gifts.

For the many occasions where only a brief prayer is requested or appropriate why not use the collect form? It can be carefully thought out and even written beforehand, it is short and not hard to memorize, and, if given in a tone of voice which is deep and low but not affected, which is reverent and yet not unnatural, in a setting of silence and in an unhurried tempo of deep expectancy, it may move people more than a sermon. People will say: "I'm not a very religious person, but, some way, when that man prays I feel sure that he is talking to God!"

The conduct of funerals is the next most frequent special occasion when the minister has a chance to lead into a worship experience people who may never darken the door of his church as well as help and comfort those who are among the saints of Zion. Here sincere religious faith and human sympathy, simplicity and brevity are the key words. A funeral, when conducted by a minister, should be a worship experience for all who are present. It is God and his sustaining care, his love for all his children, on which we must rest for strength and comfort in hours when we are baffled and bereaved. The funeral service must make that God so real by scripture and by prayer, that those who hear will say with Job: "Yea, though he slay me, yet will I trust him." The minister must help people to feel that, if it is good to be born, it is also, in God's gracious providence, good to die! "We brought nothing into this world and it is certain we can carry nothing out" is cold comfort and only very superficially true. We brought into this world marvelous personalities capable of deep enrichment. Our birth was not apart from the wisdom and love of God. Religious faith believes that death is just as much a part of life as birth is and therefore just as thoroughly undergirded by the love of God as birth is. And so we cry with the poets, "Trust God, see all, nor be afraid!" "Man was made to go on, and not to stop!"

Some such attitude of mind as that the minister seeks to establish at a funeral. All else is secondary—all information about the deceased, although it may be very proper upon occasion; and all recognition of service rendered the community, though that too may be due and fitting if it was real service, and the minister speaks from knowledge of it and what he says is poised and justified rather than fulsome or undeserved. Much depends on the judgment of the minister, his sense of what is decent and appropriate, his earlier talks with the bereaved family and his voice and manner. He must not be so solemn as to be lugubrious or so cheerful as to seem untouched by sorrow. His voice should not be filled with tears nor calculated to draw tears from others. It should have the quiet resonance of faith and courage and the warmth of hope and human sympathy.

One very important thing the minister must learn about funerals and that is the importance of taking charge of the situation, gaining emotional control over it, at the very start and retaining it to the end. This he does largely by his bearing and his voice. Hence he should beware of the funereal type of singing which will largely neutralize the atmosphere of quiet courageous faith he wishes the service to create. For this reason, except for instrumental music, he should always begin the service, strike the keynote as it were, with his own voice, generally by repeating a brief reverent invocation and then great passages from the Bible, verses from the 103rd Psalm, the 14th chapter of John, the 15th chapter First Corinthians and others of like character. In this way he secures the attention of those present and lifts the whole occasion into the region of religious faith. After this there may be an organ interlude, or a strong uplifting hymn sung as a solo or by a group of singers, then may come whatever the minister feels moved to say that will be helpful and reassuring, then the prayer, another hymn and the benediction. Such a simple service need not take over fifteen or twenty minutes, and yet not lack at all in dignity, appropriateness and human sympathy.

It is of the nature of religion that people turn to it to touch with beauty, meaning and mystery the great crises of life like birth and death and marriage. When it comes to weddings, therefore, the minister should not fail to realize why he is invited to be present. He is not there just to "officiate" or "read the lines" or "perform the ceremony"—all those familiar phrases are understatements. He is there to make the wedding a religious experience. Unless he does that a justice of the peace would have done quite as well, maybe better, if he had a sonorous voice and was a benign old character with spectacles, a shock of gray hair, a ruddy complexion and a fatherly demeanor!

How the minister shall bring a nervous groom, a self-conscious bride, a conglomeration of relatives and guests, many of them in a tittering or appraising or even cynical frame of mind, into an experience of religion in the few brief moments of the marriage ceremony, is a task for all the liturgical skill he has. And yet, unless the marriage ceremony is a deep experience of religion, the minister has failed to justify his presence. Here, as so often in his public services, his voice is the key to the situation. If he wears a gown and is obviously garbed for his part as carefully as the bride and groom are for theirs, and if his voice takes command of the situation at once, the service is off to a good start. The minister's voice should be neither faint nor booming, neither professionally unreal nor casually conversational. Its tones should give to all a sense of sincerity and reality, of tenderness without sentimentality and strength without harshness.

It will also help to create and maintain a religious atmosphere if one of the great historic marriage forms is used. Personally I prefer that of the Episcopal prayer book, with some slight modifications. The phrases of this great service are woven into the literature and thinking of English-speaking people everywhere. It has reasonable brevity and great dignity. To add a note of human appreciation I am accustomed to substitute for the prayers in this service, the following one:

O God, our Heavenly Father, the giver of every good and perfect gift, we thank thee for the supreme gift of love, whereby thou hast set the solitary in families and placed us together in beautiful human relations as fathers and mothers and children, as brothers and sisters, as husbands and wives, as friends. We invoke thy blessing on this man and this woman whom we bless in thy name. Grant that they shall surely keep and perform the vows which they have this day entered into. May thy blessing rest upon them as they go out into life now, hand in hand, together. Keep them in all their ways. May they be thy ways, full of peace and joy. And if the day come when skies must be over-clouded, grant to them in all sorts of weather that, loving and being loved, blessing and being blessed, they may find life ever filled with a deeper harmony as they no longer live it alone but learn more perfectly to share it together through the years. And so may thy blessing and the benediction of thy love rest upon the home which here is founded and grant that these twain shall be no longer twain but one. Through Jesus Christ, our Lord. Amen.

From time to time the minister will have a share, often a leading responsibility, in some service of dedication. It may be the dedication of a church, or a parish house, or an organ or a public institution like a hospital or even a private home. Happily there are now available admirably worked out services for all these occasions and I need do nothing more than refer the reader to an admirable little book which contains them, and a vast additional store of other good liturgical material as well, Thirkield and Huckel's *Book of Common Worship*, published in 1932 by E. P. Dutton and Company, New York.

But there are services in dedication of individuals, such as confirmation, joining the church and ordination, concerning which some comments and suggestions may be useful. I use the word confirmation to describe the reception of young people, usually a group of them, into the church after a period of instruction in a pastor's class preparatory to church membership. In such a class over a period of weeks or even months, they have been discussing the basic points in Christian belief and living, and now comes the hour for public allegiance to Jesus Christ and full membership in his church. It is unfortunate that in many churches, when this climactic hour comes, the young people find themselves just herded together with a group of adults coming in largely by letter. Why should there not be a special service for the young people of the communicant's class, and for them alone, at which the ritual shall be appropriate to their age and the course they have covered? How deeply impressive if, as they all kneel as a group in the chancel of the church, the pastor who has instructed them passes among them, laying his hand reverently on the head of each in turn and, using again the Christian name given in baptism, says: "N.——— I receive you into the Christian church. Defend, O Lord, this thy servant with thy heavenly grace; that he may continue thine forever, and daily increase in the knowledge of thy Holy Spirit until he come into thy everlasting Kingdom. Amen." If more than five or six are to be confirmed, only the first sentence need be used for each individual, the prayer being said as a closing benediction upon them all.

The form for receiving members into the fellowship of the church is, of course, a prescribed ritual in some denominations. But in others it is left to the minister's discretion. Many of the forms used for this occasion separate those coming on confession of faith from others coming by letter in such a way that it is sometimes a little awkward or embarrassing, especially when, for example, only one is joining on confession of faith and several by letter. Another infelicity is the requirement for members of the local church to rise in welcome to the new members, leaving seated in the pews in a somewhat anomalous situation many loyal and devoted Christians who do not happen to be members of the local congregation. To overcome these difficulties here is a brief ritual for the reception of members which unites all who are joining the church into one group regardless of whether they are being received by letter or on confession of faith, and which also calls upon all Christian people to rise as representing not only this local church but the whole universal church in welcoming these new members. This ritual is as follows:

A RITUAL FOR THE RECEPTION OF MEMBERS
INTO THE CHURCH

The Invitation

(After reading the names of those whom the church has voted to receive on confession of faith and by letter from other churches, and requesting them to come forward, the minister says:)

"Wherewith shall I come before the Lord and bow myself before the high God? . . . He hath showed thee, O man, what is good; and what doth the Lord require of thee but to do justly, to love kindness and to walk humbly with thy God." "With the heart man believeth unto righteousness and with the mouth confession is made unto salvation." "Jesus said, Whosoever shall confess me before men, him will I confess also before my Father who is in Heaven."

The Church Covenant

(Baptism having been administered to those who are not already baptized, the minister addresses all the candidates:)

Dearly beloved: Confessing, or renewing, your faith in God and your loyalty and devotion to Jesus Christ, you now enter into the membership of this church, seeking the guidance of the Holy Spirit into all truth. You covenant and engage to walk with us in the fellowship of the gospel and in all the ways of the Lord made known or to be made known to you. You take this church to be your church, promising, so far as in you lies, to share in its work, sustain its worship, love its members and seek its unity, purity and increase: You so covenant?

Response: I do.

The Response by the Church

(The members of this church, and all other churches, will please rise.)

We then affectionately welcome you as members with us of the church of Christ. We share with you its work and worship and world-wide vision. We extend to you the faith and fellowship of the universal church and pledge to you our Christian love and comradeship.

The Right Hand of Fellowship

(Here the minister gives the right hand of fellowship to each new member with such scripture verse or other words as he may choose, closing with these words as a benediction:)

And now may the God of peace make you perfect in every good work to do his will, working in you that which is well pleasing unto him, through Jesus Christ, our Lord, Amen.

Another form of personal dedication, less frequent than that of a layman joining the church but of great importance for the continuance of the church, is the rite of ordination to the Christian ministry. Surely here is a ceremonial which should be performed with the utmost of dignity, solemnity and beauty. There should be nothing casual, stupid or commonplace about an occasion where a young man's life is being set aside for the great tasks and responsibility of the Christian ministry. Some denominations have the ritual for this occasion all worked out in complete detail, but among others there is no set form beyond certain more or less binding traditions.

Those who have no fixed ritual of ordination may therefore be interested in the following one which was worked out along the general lines of the Congregational tradition but which would be equally usable, with slight adaptation, in any protestant church. This service is supposed to occur, normally, in the evening, following an ecclesiastical council held that afternoon or at some earlier date, at which the candidate for ordination has been examined and approved. The ordination vows have been made religious rather than

theological in their emphasis and have sought to forecast
the actual work of a Christian minister rather than set up
a test of ecclesiastical conformity. It is expected that the
major part of the congregation will be members of the
church to which the ordinand will minister and one object
of the service, therefore, is to join them and their young
minister together in a common ideal of Christian life and
service.

A SERVICE OF ORDINATION

Organ Prelude
Procesional Hymn

(Here the ministers who are to participate in the service march
in, following the choir, the candidate coming last, beside the moderator, but stopping at the front pew and remaining there until
the prayer of ordination.)

Statement by the Moderator

(A brief report of the findings of the ecclesiastical council au-
thorizing the ordination. The moderator then states that from here
on the service will proceed without announcement, printed or mimeographed programs being in the hands of the congregation.)

Invocation and the Lord's Prayer
Scripture Reading

(Luke 4:14-22a, is appropriate, or II Tim. 4:1-7 or some other
passage selected by the one who is to preach the sermon.)

Anthem, solo or hymn
Sermon

(This should be brief, never over one-half hour long and, if
possible, only twenty or twenty-five minutes. It should deal with
some central theme of the Christian message, particularly as related to the ministry, such as "Walking With God Today," "The
Graciousness of Jesus," "Speaking Truth in Love" or "A Prophetic Ministry" or some like theme.)

Hymn
The Vows of Ordination

(Read by the Moderator standing in the pulpit or in the center of the chancel, the candidate standing on the floor of the church facing him.)

Moderator: N——, presenting yourself for ordination to the Christian Ministry, and trusting God to help you, do you accept as your own the ideals and principles of Jesus; and do you promise, through reading, prayer, and study, to seek the continued guidance of the Holy Spirit into an ever larger knowledge of the truth?

Candidate: I do.

Moderator: Do you accept the government and fellowship of the [Congregational Churches], and promise to be a faithful minister in the work of these Churches for the service of mankind and the upbuilding of the Kingdom of God throughout the world?

Candidate: I do.

Moderator: And do you here dedicate your life to teach and preach the Christian Gospel, to exalt righteousness, to rebuke evil, to reclaim the erring, to help the poor, to uplift the fallen, to minister to the sick, to comfort those in trouble, to guide and inspire youth, and to serve your fellow men in the spirit of the Master?

Candidate: I do.

The Congregation: We, then, the people of this Church and the members of this Council, in testimony of this high purpose, do now solemnly set you apart for the work of the Christian Ministry, pledging you our love, our prayers, and our steadfast cooperation, that we may walk together in all the ways of the Lord made known, or to be made known, unto us. Amen.

The Prayer of Ordination

(This is the high point of the ceremony. Ordination is actually effected in the prayer. The candidate should kneel before the communion table, all the ministers in the chancel being grouped around him. Near the close of the prayer they will all lay their hands on his head, in accordance with ancient Christian tradition.

There should be a soft but impressive response chanted as the prayer ends. "Bless the Lord, O my Soul" by Ippolitoff-Ivanoff is suggested.

At the conclusion of the prayer the ordinand takes a seat which has been reserved for him in the chancel. The following prayer, written for Morrison's Pastor's Manual may indicate the type of prayer to be made, but it will be much better if the prayer is really made and not just read.)

O God, our heavenly Father, who art also the God of the living church and the loving heart: send Thy benediction, we pray Thee, upon this Thy servant whom we set aside this day for the work of the Christian ministry. Ordain him to Thine own service and make him wholly Thine. Quicken within him an abiding sensitivity to Thy presence, that he may ever live not in himself but in Thee. Deepen his sense of fellowship with all sorts and conditions of men and give him an understanding heart, that he may minister to all troubled souls and open to them the doors of peace.

Make him a prophet of Thy truth, O Lord, seeing clearly and speaking bravely, without hatred, bitterness or fear, but ever with his face turned toward the morning of a better day. May every cause of righteousness and brotherhood be stronger for his ministry. Help him to bring wider horizons of sympathy and social vision to all who hear him. Use him as a bugle call to justice and good will.

Send him forth, we pray Thee, an architect and builder of the universal church, lofty as is the love of God and ample as the needs of man. Above all races, creeds and nations give him the vision of universal peace and brotherhood that the kingdom of God may come close to men because of him.

To this end we pray that he may walk very close to Jesus Christ, his Saviour and the Lord and Bishop of his soul, that, whatever else men may think or say of him, they may take note that he has been with Jesus. So shall he be ordained indeed a minister of Christ and servant of the most high God; in Jesus' name. **Amen.**
The Charge to the Candidate

(This should be given by a brother minister, or some layman

may do it, and it should not ruin the atmosphere of the occasion, as is too frequently done, by an unfortunate impression that the time has now come to introduce an element of comic relief! The place for jokes and story telling is around the table at the ordination supper but the ordination service itself should not be let down in its concluding moments by any straining after humor. If humor comes naturally and without cheapening the situation, it may be all very well but it takes a real artist not to violate good taste in this regard. Hence the charge to the candidate should be serious, practical, inspiring and brief. The sermon has already been preached! This is not the time to preach another one. He who stays within five minutes will be more appreciated than the rambler who consumes fifteen.)

The Charge to the People

(Another minister or a qualified layman gives this, and the same warning that has just been sounded applies here as well. It is no time for cheap wit but rather for deepening the sense of mutual love and responsibility between pastor and people.)

The Right Hand of Fellowship

(Here a brother minister welcomes the newly ordained man into the fellowship of the local association and the ministry at large with a few well-chosen words, indicating the dignity and challenge of the ministerial calling. This also ought not to exceed five minutes.)

Recessional Hymn
Benediction

(By the newly ordained minister, and let us hope he knows one of the great benedictions of the church and repeats it accurately!)

Organ Postlude

The liturgical effectiveness of this service of ordination will depend, primarily, on the deep sense of its seriousness and solemnity by all participating in it; and, secondarily, on certain details, some of which are as follows:

1. If possible, the choir and all the participants should

be gowned. Those having hoods may dignify the occasion by wearing them.

2. Two candles burning on the communion table, unless the table is in line between the pulpit and the congregation.

3. No announcements as the service proceeds.

4. Carefully chosen appropriate music and hymns.

5. Brevity and careful preparation by those participating.

6. Making sure those invited to take part will really do so, thus avoiding substitutions.

7. Making clear to congregation and community in advance the significance of the occasion and the interesting character of the program, so that the church may be well filled with a sympathetic and cooperating congregation.

One form of public worship services which deserves to be fully explored and developed in a book by itself is the worship in camps, summer conferences and on vacation occasions generally. With people more and more leaving their settled abodes behind them in the summer, together with such church-going habits as they may possess, the provision of worship, outdoors or under quite unecclesiastical conditions in the summer vacation season, presents a challenging problem to the church. But it is a challenge which contains within it a great opportunity. One need only look in upon some of our young peoples camps and summer conferences to be impressed with the fact that here is a vital experiment station in Christian worship. The very unconventionality of the surroundings drives the leaders of public worship under such circumstances back to first principles and may well result in interesting new developments.

One final topic remains, however, in connection with the

occasional services which a minister is called upon to render: Should he accept fees for performing them? If eating a dinner and sitting through half a dozen speeches afterward, is a fee for saying grace on certain occasions it is probably well earned! The minister's fee at a wedding is a custom too well established to disturb! Why disturb it, anyway, since the fee goes not to the minister but to the minister's wife? Where a man is at expense of time and travel to render some particular service he may properly receive special remuneration. But no minister would wish to receive any payment for assisting in the ordination of a brother minister, or performing a baptism. With regard to funerals, also, the question may be raised if the minister does well to accept fees. Would not his influence in the community be much stronger if he quietly took this position: I am here as a minister supported by the church to render pastoral service to my church and community in time of need. Death often brings harassing financial problems into the home. It is, therefore, my joy and privilege to let it be known that the services of a minister and the consolations of religion at such a time and under all circumstances are without money and without price. My own personal experience justifies such a stand. Where no money is exchanged, one receives in honor, love and gratitude what is far more precious and one helps to lift the church above any accusation of being mercenary.

Worship and Preaching

"If I can add any distinctness to your idea of God, any beauty to your notion of virtue; if I can represent the life of Christ in such vivid and true colors as to exalt your love; if I can persuade one young man to check the running tide of sensual pleasure by the force of moral obligation; if I can prevail with one old man to forgive an injury that has rankled in his breast till hatred has grown into habit, out of regard to the example of Jesus and his law of love; if I can arrest one angry sarcasm of wounded pride in the moment of irritation, one syllable of slander as it trembles on the tongue, by the memory of the motives I have called to your aid; if a sermon of mine shall be remembered as a solace in the chamber of sorrow, if when the eye of one of you is closing forever on this world, your spirit, as it passes, shall thank me for one triumphant hope, —then, my brethren, it is praise enough, then I shall bless God that I have not been wholly wanting to his cause, that, by me, one mite is added to the sum of happiness." [1]

These words represent the ideals of a young minister and form the closing paragraph of a sermon preached on the Sunday following his ordination. They were written by Ralph Waldo Emerson in 1829! He was then a young man

[1] *Young Emerson Speaks*, a collection of sermons by Ralph Waldo Emerson edited by Arthur Cushman McGiffert. Houghton Mifflin Co. 1937, p. 30.

of twenty-five, just beginning his three-year pastorate at
the Second Church in Boston. A reading of the sermon at
the close of which these words occur will reveal that the
youthful Emerson had preaching primarily in mind as the
means by which the service so nobly summarized was to
be rendered.

But we know today that preaching is not enough. This is
not to discount preaching, and certainly no counsel to neglect it. But preaching is not really preaching, it is only a
form of oratory or, at best, of religious public speech, until
it is set in the midst of worship and made radiant with the
light which worship may throw upon it. Preaching may do
much for worship. It ought to plow so deep into human
self-complacency as to arouse a deep sense of contrition. It
ought to make God so real and inescapable as to sow the
seeds of personal devotion and dauntless faith. It ought to
arouse a will to nobler action so resolute as to reap at last
a harvest of fruitful service to the Kingdom of God. But, in
all these things, preaching is incomplete. It only prepares
the way for that personal adjustment to God and commitment to do God's will which is actually consummated only
in the sanctuary of worship. It is worship that registers in
the soul and in the presence of God the noblest moods and
aspirations which the preacher can arouse. Hence the sermon on one Sunday may make the worship which has preceded it more meaningful and also prepare the way for a
deeper worship experience on the Sundays that are to
follow.

On the other hand, worship may do much for preaching.
It prepares the congregation for the sermon by taking them
beforehand on an excursion to heavenly places. In the

thirty or forty minutes before the sermon the worship service should have helped people turn from the landscape of their defeats and difficulties, the fog and smoke of daily living, and lift up their eyes to the mountains of God. Then, when the preacher enters the pulpit, they are ready to listen to him. Nor is it to the congregation alone that this emotional quieting and intellectually clarifying experience may come. The minister also has been prepared to preach by the very experiences of conducting public worship. He does not rush into the pulpit from the street. He stops first to gain perspective, peace and poise within his own soul. After a great worship experience it ought to be easier to preach a really great sermon, in tune with the nobility of the prayer and praise which have preceded it. If the sermon is out of tune with what has gone before, if it has spots where it is harsh, or conceited, or blatant, or cheap, the minister will be made more conscious of them and so be enabled to correct them. Worship has given him a touchstone for his preaching.

Emerson's ideal for his pastoral relationship admirably sums up both what the true-hearted minister would like to do and what undoubtedly the congregation needs, but it will take a fine balance and coordination of preaching, worship and pastoral work to accomplish it. Emerson ultimately left the pastorate. He had a genius for writing and for lecturing, but no equal talent for pastoral work. One cannot but wonder if he had adequate appreciation of the help worship might have contributed to the attainment of his ministerial ideal. In a way Emerson failed. He succeeded gloriously as an essayist and as a popular philosopher. He exerted a mighty influence on his generation and that which followed. But he apparently failed as a pastor. And he failed because, noble as his goals were, he did not have the temperament to do the work needed to attain them; and possibly, in part, because he did not have the requisite approach to the function of public worship. Preaching, even such preaching as an Emerson could do, was not enough!

These are days which demand great preaching, God knows! But, that it may be truly preaching and not just philosophizing or oratory, it needs all the more to be an integral part of a great experience of worship. No worship without preaching! That is to say preaching must always enrich the content and give direction and purpose to worship. But also, no preaching without worship! Which is to say that out of worship comes the noblest preaching endowed with spiritual insight and powers of self-criticism. It takes both worship and preaching to work the miracle of divine communion and consecration which men need so urgently today.

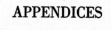

APPENDICES

Check Lists on Public Worship

1. *The Minister's Conduct of Worship*

It is hoped that the following check lists may be of value to men who want an objective way of measuring the efficiency of their conduct of public worship, and also of evaluating the music part of the service. They have been prepared by Professor Norman E. Richardson of the Presbyterian Theological Seminary in Chicago, who has done notable work in the field of religious education and in the various phases of pastoral leadership.

Professor Richardson makes the following suggestion as to the use of the first check list in which a minister is seeking to obtain an objective self-appraisal.

"There are 26 items in this check list. Under each one is a series of figures, 0, 1, 2, 3, 4, 5. Draw a circle around the figure that most nearly represents a true appraisal of current practice, assuming 5 to be a perfect score for that item. Add all the 26 numbers around which circles have been drawn. Divide this sum by 130 (the highest possible combined score for all 26 checking points). The result represents the percentage of efficiency, in the judgment of the one who has done the scoring.

"Such an appraisal contains more or less of subjective elements. Self appraisal is seldom correct. A minister who has an unwarranted superior feeling will rate his practice as an administrator of worship too high. The one afflicted with unwarranted inferiority feelings will rate his leadership too low. In order to avoid this subjective influence, it is suggested that the minister ask one or more of the trusted and intelligent members of his church, for whom worship is a vital and meaningful experience, to make independent appraisals, using this same instrument. His own judgment can thus be checked upon, objectively.

"It must be remembered, however, that diagnosis is but a preliminary step to prescription. To find out what is wrong does not, automatically, set things right. After the weaknesses have been discovered, the real task is to follow through until improvements are effected. This check list is designed as a guide to the discovery of practices that need to be changed or that can be considered satisfactory. The efforts of the minister who seeks self improvement as an administrator of public worship must be left in the hands of one who is intimately familiar with his own personality and vocational problems. This one suggestion, however, may be made. Superiority as an administrator of public worship is a goal which every gospel minister may well cherish."

HOW TO JUDGE A MINISTER AS AN ADMINISTRATOR
OF PUBLIC WORSHIP

1. As he enters the chancel or takes his place on the pulpit platform, is the minister fully prepared to administer the entire service?

   Has he anticipated every event in the service? Does he appreciate how seriously his leadership is injured if he leaves his place of leadership to get a hymn book, to consult with someone in the congregation, or to get some papers which, inadvertently, he left back in the study or office? When the time for the service to begin arrives, is he competent and ready to administer it in every detail? Is he free from the disposition to leave administrative details at loose ends?
   0 1 2 3 4 5

2. Does he appreciate the value of the historical approach to the study of both the form and the content of public worship?

   Are his own personal standards of value being enriched and chastened by intelligent familiarity with the ancient liturgies, prayers, introits, hymns, symbols, litanies, and

ceremonials by which the spiritual life of the church has been enriched, through past centuries? Is he free from liturgical zeal that is not according to historical knowledge? Does he reverence the liturgical achievements of the church during her long and eventful history?
0 1 2 3 4 5

3. Is he free from obtrusive self display and the disposition to draw attention to himself, his talents, his attire, or his own function as leader?

Are his appraisal of himself and his personal bearing aids to those who are intent upon communion with God? Has he the grace of obvious and sincere humility? Does he deflect attention from himself to God? Does his leadership glorify God?
0 1 2 3 4 5

4. In spite of inward fears and feelings of incompetency or unworthiness, is he able to carry on, as an administrator, with a personal bearing that inspires confidence?

To play his part as leader may not be easy. Consciousness of lack of natural endowment or of the superiority of certain people present in the congregation may act as a heavy handicap. But is the minister faithful and sincere in doing his best to fill his high office, trusting God, implicitly, for help in time of need? Does he realize how ready and able God is to help him?
0 1 2 3 4 5

5. Is he personally "en rapport" with his surroundings?

Is he in harmony with the atmosphere of the sanctuary, the spirit of the Lord's Day, the order of worship, the spiritual aspirations and needs of the people, the best traditions of public worship? Is he free from conscious attitudes and from mannerisms that suggest incongruity with the recognized presence of God? Does he appreciate the fact that he is dealing with dedicated things? Is his own reverence obvious?

0 1 2 3 4 5

6. Is his personal attire fitting and useful in view of his personality and sacred vocation?

Is he dressed in some fashion that is distinctive of his vocation? Do his clothes symbolize his leadership in worship? Does he feel the support and social protection of garments that suggest to himself and to the congregation the sacredness and uniqueness of his office? Is his wearing apparel in keeping with the total setting of the service?

0 1 2 3 4 5

7. Does he maintain an attitude of cordial, sensitive cooperation with all who assist him as leaders?

Is there mutual understanding and intelligent appreciation between him and the ushers, the organist, the choir master, the choir, the assisting minister, the sexton, the collectors of the offering, the hospitality committee, and all others who hold positions of special responsibility? Is there unity of purpose and procedure among all who, in specialized ways, help to make the service an event of deep spiritual significance?

0 1 2 3 4 5

8. Before the service begins, does he, by prayer, consecrate himself and dedicate all others who participate in it as leaders with him, to their holy offices?

When the service is about to begin, does he intercede for the members of the choir and for other leaders, in their presence, praying that all may have special grace in meeting their respective responsibilities? Do all enter the sanctuary in the spirit of prayer and with a consciousness of God's presence?

0 1 2 3 4 5

9. Is his administration of the service motivated by a well-balanced passion to save the lost and to foster spiritual growth?

Has he confidence in worship as a means of carrying forward God's total plan of redemption, conservation, and perfection of those who bear the divine image and, also, as a means of fostering and conserving the corporate spiritual life of the church? Are the services planned for the purpose of achieving both evangelistic and educational results?

0 1 2 3 4 5

10. Does he show good taste and a keen sense of proportion in his selection and arrangement of the materials used in each worship service?

Is he open to suggestion and does he make use of ideas contributed by musicians, ushers, and others who help him in the service? Is he constantly seeking how to improve the worship services? Does he have ideals that are well balanced with regard to the use of music, prayer, scripture, sermon, and all other elements that constitute the service?

0 1 2 3 4 5

11. Is he careful to avoid making reference to persons, to himself, to members of the congregation, or to others, when such reference interferes with worship?

If reference is made to persons, is it concerned with their relationship to God or to their religious significance? Are inconsequential and frivolous matters avoided? If it is necessary for him to call attention to the need of ventilation does he do it unobtrusively? If persons are referred to in the announcements, is this done respectfully?

0 1 2 3 4 5

12. Are his sermons constituted and delivered with definite reference to the entire worship service?

Are they well regulated in regard to length? Are their contents or subject matter integrated with the other features of the service? Do they generate spiritual vitality and are they wholesomely regenerative, without being detached from or incongruous with the other elements in the order of worship? Are they reverent and worshipful in spirit? Do they reflect a lofty and inspiring point of view? Are they saturated with God consciousness? Are they the product of a devout, quiet, and studious mind?

0 1 2 3 4 5

13. Is he sympathetically aware of the changing emphases included in the Christian year?

Is he resourceful in planning and administering the yearly cycle of worship, including the great Christian festivals of Christmas, Good Friday, Easter, and Whitsunday? Does he make the most of attitudes that are current in the community and that can be used to give special tones or qualities to the worship services? Does he relate the services, helpfully, to the current events in which the members of the congregation are interested?

0 1 2 3 4 5

14. Is he particularly considerate of music and those who provide the musical features of the service?

Is his cooperation intelligently appreciative of music as an aid in creating and expressing truly religious sentiments? Does he set a good example in hymn singing? Does he avoid using the time while the congregation is singing, to attend to other administrative matters? Have he and the organist and choir master considered, together, the musical features of the service?

0 1 2 3 4 5

15. While administering the service, is he protected from the approaches of those who have announcements to be made or suggestions which they wish to make to him personally?

Does he, tactfully, let his people know that after he has entered the pulpit platform or the chancel and has begun the public administration of the service, he is averse to making and recognizing social contacts? Does he maintain sufficient social detachment to make his leadership effective?

0 1 2 3 4 5

16. Is he a substantial and reliable source of interesting information and fruitful knowledge concerning religious matters?

As a religious leader, is he well informed? Do his people respect him as a source of spiritually quickening information? Is he an alert, diligent student, familiar with the new bodies of knowledge which are so abundantly available in an age of research experimentation and discovery? Are his contributions richly meaningful?

0 1 2 3 4 5

17. Does he have a well-organized "source book of worship"?

Is he alert to observe and evaluate materials, including printed or mimeographed orders of worship used in other churches, clippings from current publications, new hymns, prayers, and litanies for use on special occasions? Does he keep these materials systematically assembled for use, as occasions arise? Can he locate them readily?

0 1 2 3 4 5

18. Does his library contain well-selected books and other materials on worship?

Is he a student of hymnody, symbolism, dramatics, the historical creeds of the faith, the psychology of worship, ecclesiastical architecture, and other subjects that are vitally related to worship? Is he sincerely interested in the theory, history, and practice of worship? Does he own a substantial collection of hymnals for use in church, church

school and young people's societies? Does his library reflect discriminative taste?

0 1 2 3 4 5

19. Is he sufficiently dramatic and forceful in his administration
of the order of worship to capture and hold the attention of
the congregation?

Is his personality released and strong? Does he measure
up to the requirements of a leader of group worship? In
voice and personal bearing, is he sufficiently expressive?
Does his personal influence reach those in the sanctuary
who are farthest from him?

0 1 2 3 4 5

20. Does he challenge the respect and confidence of the most
and, also, the least intelligent and cultured members of the
congregation?

Is he free from the weakness of talking or praying over the
heads of his people? Can he express himself in simple
language? Does he use concepts that can be comprehended
by all? Does he avoid the appearance of striving to be
"learned" or egotistically superior?

0 1 2 3 4 5

21. Is he free from personality tensions and prejudices that in-
terfere with good judgment concerning religious matters and
with versatility in the administration of worship?

Does he have a point of view and general attitude that ap-
proximates that of Jesus Christ? Has he the mind of
Christ,—with strong, fixed convictions, yet capable of
changing moods? Is he trustworthy, poised, honorable,
and resourceful in handling the worship activities of his
church?

0 1 2 3 4 5

22. Does he read the scriptures well and does he handle the
pulpit Bible properly?

Is his use of the Bible an integral and worthy part of the service? Does he open and close it appropriately? Is his reading of the Bible intelligently and sympathetically interpretative? As he reads, do the members of the congregation realize that they are listening to the word of God?

0 1 2 3 4 5

23. Are the prayers which he offers, as part of the worship service, helpful to the members of the congregation as they hold communion with God?

Are they sincere, expressed in appropriate language, and clearly differentiated in form and purpose,—expressing gratitude, contrition, dedication, adoration, intercession, contemplation, petition, consecration, and other appropriate attitudes? Do they reflect a clear consciousness of the congregation and of God? Are they well regulated in the matter of length?

0 1 2 3 4 5

24. Is he free from the unconscious conceit which assumes that a service that is suited to his own needs, interests, and understanding is thereby well adapted to meet the needs of others, whose personalities are different from his own?

Has he the social imagination, intelligent sympathy, and educational insight needed to prepare and administer services of worship primarily for the congregation of which he is minister? Can he keep them, individually and collectively, in mind while planning each service? Is he both objective and sincere as he prepares services of worship for others?

0 1 2 3 4 5

25. Does he, personally, sustain a worshipful attitude throughout the service?

Does he participate in it as though it were his own service? Does he, also, worship vicariously as the accredited leader of his people? As he worships, does he feel that virtue

goes out of him? Is he aware of the common needs of himself and the congregation, for worship?
0 1 2 3 4 5

26. Does he try, specifically, to create conditions that are favorable for the manifestation of God to his people?

Is he consciously working with the Holy Spirit, using worship as a means of helping the worshipers to live spiritually eventful and progressively spiritual lives? Does he administer the service in confidence that God will use it to further His own purpose in the personalities and lives of the worshipers and of the church? Does his administration of worship reflect a strong faith in worship as an occasion when God's presence can be realized and recognized?
0 1 2 3 4 5

SUPPLEMENTARY ITEM

If the minister is so unfortunate as to be defective in his appreciation of and ability to use music, rhythm, or other aesthetic values, does he try to make up for his defects by securing the cooperation of those who have not been thus deprived?

There are certain defects of personality such as color blindness; difficulty of hearing; defective sense of harmony, pitch, melody; and lack of appreciation of superior literary values that are heavy handicaps in the administration of worship. If a minister is thus afflicted, he should face the facts, objectively, and see to it that some one is standing by, ready at all times to make up for his deficiency. A minister who is blind or deaf or seriously maimed should give serious consideration to the question of his fitness to administer public worship.

2. The Use of Music in Public Worship

Professor Richardson makes the following suggestions for guidance in the use of the check list which follows:

"It is suggested that copies of this check list be read by all members of the church and congregation who are interested in sacred music, instrumental or vocal, whether as soloists or as members of a choir or an orchestra. Soon, thereafter, let all such persons, under the leadership of the minister and the choir master, attend a meeting for the purpose of laying plans for the improvement of the musical features of the services of public worship in which they are interested.

"The musical features of the worship services can be studied and evaluated with reference to each one of the 22 checking points included in this list. The percentage of efficiency in using music to facilitate worship, may be ascertained in the following manner: Draw a circle around the number that most nearly represents how near to perfection (5 is a perfect score) your public worship services come, when judged from the standpoint of each one of the 22 items. The highest possible score is 5 times 22 or 110. The score for your church is found by adding the 22 numbers around which you have drawn circles and dividing by 110. The total score is the percentage of efficiency of your services of public worship when evaluated with reference to their musical features. These appraisals, made by individuals, independently of each other, can be made the basis of group discussion at this first meeting.

"It should not be assumed that this list is an infallible guide for making an appraisal of the musical aspects of services of public worship, much less, for the services in their entirety. Before a reliable plan for their improvement can be drawn up or a definite policy can be adopted with safety, it may be necessary to make use of the other check lists."

CHECKING UP ON THE USE OF MUSIC IN PUBLIC WORSHIP

1. Does the music glorify God? Is it interpretative of the attributes of God?

   Is it religious in the sense that it helps people to direct their thinking toward the Creator and Ruler of the uni-

verse? Is it free from suggestions that are obtrusively irreligious? In composition and performance, or interpreta-
tation, are all instrumental and vocal selections worthy of
use in a service that is intended to inspire people as they
express praise and adoration to God or dedication to the
fulfillment of His divine purpose? Is it distinctively religious,—free from secularism?
0 1 2 3 4 5

2. Are the musicians intelligently sensitive with regard to their
function in the service?

Are they consecrated to the task of helping people to realize the presence of God and to hold communion with Him?
Do they oppose the use of music to glorify the composer or
those who interpret it by voice or instrument, or primarily
to display the possibilities or special features of the instrument used? Are the personalities of the musicians properly
hidden in the message and contribution of the music to the
service? Are they free from selfish ambition, desire for
social recognition, or eagerness for a demonstration of
musical ability? Can they deflect attention from themselves
to God or to the word of God?
0 1 2 3 4 5

3. Do the hymns used in each service facilitate the progress or
movement of the service?

Are they interpretative of the unfolding theme or pattern
of the service? Are they vitally related to other elements in
the service that are placed before and after them? Are they
used appropriately to open and close the services or to
emphasize particular events in the cycle of worship experiences included in the service?
0 1 2 3 4 5

4. Are all the hymns, in both text and tune, worthy of use in
public worship?

Do they serve the purpose of expressing man's noblest aspirations and loftiest sentiments? Are they an aid to the
kind of worship in which communion with God is central?
Are they free from vulgar or irreligious associations? Are
they well distributed with reference to the great epochs in
the history of Christian hymnody?
0 1 2 3 4 5

5. Is due respect shown for each hymn and musical composition
   in its original form or as its author intended it to be used?

   Is the unity or integrity of each hymn preserved? Are the
   hymns protected from mutilation by having stanzas omitted
   when the omission injures the real message and literary
   unity of the texts? Are the hymns protected from being
   used to fill in gaps in the service or to kill time?
   0 1 2 3 4 5

6. Is the universal character of Christian hymnody appreciated
   by both minister and people?

   Its outreach, bridging across the centuries, the sectarian
   divisions and national or racial barriers? Is hymnody—
   the structure, history, meaning, and use of hymns, of vital
   interest to the members of the choir and to the worshipers?
   Is the church free from that spiritual provincialism which
   insists upon singing over and over again, a relatively small
   number of "old favorites" and which resents the use of
   unfamiliar hymns, no matter how appropriate they may be?
   0 1 2 3 4 5

7. Do the hymns and responses win intelligent appreciation and
   hearty use by the members of the congregation?

   Does their use bring satisfaction and lofty enjoyment? Do
   they help personalities in the choir and congregation to
   become released and expressive? Are the worshipers glad
   to express the sentiments embodied in them? Do all the
   musicians, including the organist, the choir master, the
   members of the choir, and the members of the music com-

mittee, appreciate what music can do for human personalities when its rhythm, harmony and melody facilitate true worship? Does the total range of music used in the worship services of the church, include whatever is required to meet the interests, needs, and capacities of children, adolescents, adults, and senescents?

0 1 2 3 4 5

8. Is the music consistent with the general setting of the worship service?

If the service is simple, is the music characterized by simplicity? If the service is elaborate, is the music correspondingly rich in artistic quality? Is it carefully balanced with the other features of the services, free from the disposition to "steal the show," to make itself unduly conspicuous or not conspicuous enough?

0 1 2 3 4 5

9. Under the leadership of the choir, the organ (piano), and the minister, does the entire congregation worship through the use of hymns?

Are the hymns sung in proper tempo? Are the printed instructions in the hymnal concerning interpretation or manner of rendering followed? Are hymn singing and the use of musical responses vital parts of the participation of the congregation in worship? Have the best hymnals available been provided?

0 1 2 3 4 5

10. Are the special musical numbers so constituted and rendered that the members of the congregation consider them to be integral and appropriate parts of the order of worship?

Are they free from mere entertainment or theatrical features? Have they sufficient merit to warrant their being used in the service? Are they free from art for art's sake, alone? Do the artists make a vital but impersonal con-

tribution to the worship experiences of the members of the congregation?
0 1 2 3 4 5

11. Is music used effectively to cover up the mechanics of the services?

These include interludes when late comers are being seated, the retirement of children who participate in the early part of the services, the serving of the elements in Communion, transitions from one event to another in the order of worship. Does music help to make the service continuous— free from interruptions and distractions?
0 1 2 3 4 5

12. Are the mechanics of the music successfully hidden?

Is the choir well disciplined? Is it unified? Are the tuning of instruments, adjustment or use of vestments, snapping on and off of organ motor, turning lights on and off, organist sliding on and off the bench, the activities of the choir director, the distribution and collection of music used by choir and the orchestra, the appearance or retirement of musicians, all as inconspicuous as possible?
0 1 2 3 4 5

13. Are the musicians careful not to constitute distractions from worship?

By restlessness, whispered social conversation, chewing gum, passing notes, failure to participate in the service, inattentiveness during the service, or unduly conspicuous personal attire or behavior. Do they realize how discourteous it is for them to retire from the sanctuary immediately after they have made their particular contribution to the service or before the entire service has been concluded? Do they refrain from smiling or frowning at each other when mistakes are made?
0 1 2 3 4 5

14. Are the musical instruments, including the organ, in good repair and worthy of use in the services?

Do the musicians take good care of their instruments, reporting, promptly, conditions that call for repair? Is the music committee alert and sensitive regarding its duty in supplying good instruments and in keeping the instruments in good repair? Are they mindful of children and young people in the congregation who have musical talent but cannot afford instruments or training?

0 1 2 3 4 5

15. Whenever vocal music is being accompanied by an organ or piano, does the accompanist confine his playing to merely adequate support for the singers?

Is his playing so controlled that it does not overpower, obscure, or overshadow them? Does the player interpret and adapt all registration designations of the music with definite reference to the size of the instrument, the acoustical properties of the sanctuary, the strength of the voices, and the size of the congregation? Is inappropriate use of the tremolo stop avoided?

0 1 2 3 4 5

16. Are members of the congregation having musical talent encouraged to qualify for leadership and honored service in this field?

As far as possible are the musicians selected from the membership of the church? Does the church encourage young musicians to become masters of sacred music? Does the church have a body or guild of musicians that mean to it what the sons of Levi meant to the Temple at Jerusalem?

0 1 2 3 4 5

17. Are the musical features of the service in keeping with the skill or ability of the musicians?

Church music may be classified as "easy," "moderately difficult," and "difficult." Musicians should exercise care in their choice of the selections which they undertake to use. Rather have a moderately difficult anthem well rendered than to have a difficult one poorly interpreted.

0 1 2 3 4 5

18. Is the music on such a cultural level that members of the congregation can recognize and appreciate it?

Worship should be educational as well as devotional. Its constant improvement from the standpoint of artistic and aesthetic values should be a concern of those responsible for it. This progress, however, should not be forced. Negative reactions due to an excess of innovations, should be avoided, in all attempts to improve public worship. The new discoveries should keep pace with spiritual development.

0 1 2 3 4 5

19. Do the processional and recessional, if used, reflect special study of these features of public worship?

Do the hymns used have appropriate sentiment and strong rhythm? Are they of proper length? Does the congregation rise and join with the choir as the second stanza of the processional hymn is begun? Is the closing stanza of the recessional sung appropriately? Do the members of the choir know how to march?

0 1 2 3 4 5

20. Are the stories of the hymns and hymn writers used appropriately in helping worshipers to get a better understanding and appreciation of the hymns?

Is this information made available in various ways—sermons to children, printed in church bulletin, explained in the prayer-meetings and in various group meetings?

0 1 2 3 4 5

21. Is prayer offered at choir rehearsals?

At the close of each choir rehearsal, do members of the

choir offer intercessory prayer for the worship service in which they are to participate? Do these prayers include and go beyond the choir's own contribution to the service? Is the choir sincerely concerned about the success of the entire service?

0 1 2 3 4 5

22. Does the music committee really function?

Do the members of the committee attend choir rehearsals and speak appreciatively of the work done by the choir? Are they alert to help the choir by providing appropriate music and other equipment? Do they safeguard the item for music in the budget of the church? Are they students of church music? Do they tactfully call the attention of the organist and choir master to interesting current events and the publication of new hymns, hymnals or other musical facilities? Do they appreciate the importance of their duty and what good music can do for the spiritual life of the church?

0 1 2 3 4 5

"Musicians who assist in services of common worship should be ambitious to develop in two directions. Whatever native talent they possess suggests the need of improvement in technical skill. But mastery of the art of music, whether vocal or instrumental, is no substitute for a sympathetic, personal attitude toward worship. Musicians may well cultivate a great devotion to the sanctuary and to the ministry of worship to mankind. Skill and devotion, both, offer opportunities for continuous improvement."

H. B. SIMONDS,

Department of Music
Presbyterian Theological Seminary, Chicago

Annotated Book-List

Not a complete bibliography but rather a selection of books most likely to prove useful to the pastor who may wish to do further reading along the line of Christian Worship.

I—The Whole Field of Worship

Bradley, Dwight: *Creative Worship.*
A very brief general survey but with many wise insights and practical suggestions.

Clarke, W. K. Lowther: *Liturgy and Worship.*
An encyclopedic companion to the Anglican Prayer Book. A mine of information.

Coffin, Henry Sloane: *In a Day of Social Rebuilding.*
The chapter on "Worship" in this book is stimulating and forward-looking.

Dearmer, Percy: *The Church at Prayer, Everyman's History of the Prayer Book.*
All of Dearmer's books are eminently worthwhile but these two will be most helpful and interesting to American ministers. The author combines erudition with human insight and breadth of sympathy.

Fiske, George Walter: *The Recovery of Worship.*
The author, formerly professor at Oberlin, is as thoroughly American in outlook as Percy Dearmer is English.

Odgers and Schultz: *The Technique of Public Worship.*
Another definitely American manual by leaders toward better worship in the Methodist Church. Strong on practical details.

Ross, G. A. Johnston: *Christian Worship and Its Future.*

A fresh and original appraisal of public worship by one who, as both preacher and scholar, combined Scottish and American viewpoints.

Sclater, J. R. P.: *The Public Worship of God.*

Lyman Beecher Lectures by a wise and thoughtful Canadian pastor. Probably embodies the best in the Scotch Presbyterian tradition carried to America.

Sperry, Willard L.: *Reality in Worship.*

Probably the best all-round book on worship yet written in America. Combines insight into the underlying philosophy of worship with practical wisdom born of sound experience and all fused together in a prose style of notable charm and power.

Underhill, Evelyn: *Worship.*

A profound, scholarly and philosophical study of the inner realities of worship rather than its outward forms, by a great English mystic.

Vogt, Von Ogden: *Art and Religion.*

This book, with Sperry's, should be prescribed reading in any course on worship. A sympathetic but none-the-less modern and Protestant appraisal of the historic and artistic background of public worship.

Modern Worship. The further and more concrete application to worship of the facts and attitudes developed in his earlier book.

Will, Robert: *Le Culte.*

A mine of erudition and insight for those who read French.

II—Special Phases of Worship

Angus, S.: *Environment of Early Christianity, The Mystery Religions and Christianity.*

These books along with those of Case and Willoughby give contemporary information about previously little understood influences on Christianity from popular cults of the Graeco-Roman world.

Case, S. J.: *Evolution of Early Christianity.*

This, with other books like Streeter on *The Primitive Church* and Franz Cumont on *The Oriental Religions in Roman Paganism*, will give interesting background material.

Coulton, G. G.: *Art and the Reformation.*

So many books on liturgy and church architecture are Catholic in tendency that this book is especially valuable as a balance containing both great historical scholarship and a rugged Protestant point of view. Note especially Chapter XIII on "Symbolism."

Dearmer, Percy: *The Parson's Hand-book.*

This book is included only that anyone tempted to go too far in liturgical detail may peruse its pages, take a look into the abyss of ritualism and draw back!

Dunney, Joseph A.: *The Mass.*

Evidently written to instruct Catholic youth in an understanding of the Mass. Protestants need to know what it teaches, too.

Holme, F. Edward: *Symbolism in Christian Art.*

An old book but packed with information.

Lotz, P. H.: *The Quest for God through Worship.*

A simple, helpful book concerning worship services for young people.

Oesterley, W. O. E.: *Jewish Backgrounds of Christian Liturgy.*

Just what its title implies and very interesting.

Morrison, C. C.: *The Social Gospel and the Christian Cultus.*

An examination of the relationship of worship to the Christian social message.

Sullivan, John F.: *The Externals of the Catholic Church.*

A book which will explain and interpret to Protestants many details of Catholic worship and create more sympathetic understanding.

Webber, F. R.: *Church Symbolism.*

A great and valuable work though strongly colored by intense high-church enthusiasms.

Wieman, H. N.: *Methods of Private Religious Living.*

A book on the personal side of worship by a teacher of the philosophy and psychology of religion.

Willoughby, H. R.: *Pagan Regeneration.*
More light on the mystery religions.
Whitehead, Alfred N.: *Symbolism.*
Some of this book is not easy reading, but he who would understand worship needs to think deeply about symbolism.

III—Books of Prayers and Other Worship Material

The Book of Common Prayer (Episcopal)
The Book of Common Worship (Presbyterian)
The Prayer Book or Missal (Roman Catholic)

Alexander and Goslin: *Worship through Drama.*
Drama and interpretative dancing are a fresh and inviting field for the extension of worship experiences.
Eastman, Fred: *A Pageant of Worship.*
Holmes, John Haynes: *Readings from Great Authors.*
Selections from thirty modern and six ancient writers suitable for unison or responsive reading in worship services.
Hume, Robert E.: *Treasure House of the World's Religions.*
A collection of the noblest passages in the literature of various world religions.
Mattoon and Bragdon: *Services for the Open.*
Suggested orders of worship for use in camps and other outdoor occasions. Rich in nature poetry.
Newton, J. Fort: *Altar Stairs.*
Beautiful and uplifting prayers by a preacher of fine liturgical feeling.
Noyes, Morgan Phelps: *Prayers for Services.*
An invaluable collection of prayers, ancient and modern, gathered from many sources and edited with fine understanding. An invaluable source book for leaders of worship, probably the most standard thing of its kind.
Orchard, Wm. E.: *The Temple.*
Prayers of deep feeling written in beautiful, if sometimes a little too highly embroidered English.

Palmer, Albert W.: "Aids to Worship" section of the *Inter-Church Hymnal*.

A comprehensive collection of Biblical and extra-Biblical worship material including unison and responsive readings, prayers, litanies and responsive prayers and confessions of faith.

Rauschenbusch, Walter: *Prayers of the Social Awakening*.

Vigorous vital prayers reflecting modern social moods with a notable prose introduction on the Lord's Prayer and its social implications.

Stevenson, Robert Louis: *Vailima Prayers*.

Written for use of his inter-racial household in his island mountain home in Samoa.

Thirkield and Huckel: *Book of Common Worship*.

A Methodist bishop and Congregational parson collaborate in an admirably worked out service book. Invaluable to the working pastor.

Index

EMMANUEL
SCHOOL OF RELIGION
LIBRARY